Effective Discipline
the Montessori Way

by

Charlotte Cushman

Cover Design by Aldo Presti
Book Layout by Mark Van Horne

ISBN: 978-0-578-67854-2

Dedication

To Merthene White, my supervising teacher:
You had the patience to teach me what I needed to
know about discipline. I am forever grateful.

To our children and grandchildren:
You are loved and cherished more than you know.

To my former Montessori students:
You were enjoyed and are remembered
more than you know.

Acknowledgements

I want to thank Stephanie Van Fleet, a Montessori colleague who worked with me in my classroom for a year and now has an elementary classroom of her own, for encouraging me to speak and write about this topic, and also for her helpful feedback.

Thank you to Dan, my husband, who proofread each rough draft.

Thank you to Michael Berliner, Sunny Lohmann, Jacqueline Lehman, Edwin Locke, Ron Pisaturo, Ed Mazlish, Laura Hilse, Susan Sheridan and Peggy Jellinger for their helpful criticisms, suggestions, feedback and editing corrections.

I want to thank Gay Hartfiel of Portraits from the Heart, who took the photo that is on the back of this book. And thank you to my assistant, Stacy Garcia, and the families at Minnesota Renaissance School for giving me permission to use that photo.

At a given moment a child becomes interested in a piece of work, showing it by the expression of his face, by his intense attention, by his perseverance in the same exercise. That child has set foot upon the road leading to discipline.[1]

MARIA MONTESSORI

1 Maria Montessori, *The Montessori Reader*, (New York: Simon and Schuster, 2013), p. 252.

Table of Contents

Preface

Before I took my Montessori training, I graduated from college with a bachelor's degree in elementary education. I had always wanted to be a teacher. I loved kids and they liked me. I was always consistent with them. I said what I meant and always followed through so they listened to me. I knew how to handle children—or so I thought.

In my senior year I did my student teaching in a second grade class consisting of thirty-five children. Thirty-five. It was a lot different from dealing with one or two. When I spoke, they didn't listen. When I told them to do something, they didn't do it. When I gave them directions, they didn't follow them. The classroom was chaos. The children didn't respect me. It wasn't fun. I was floundering.

There were no classes in college that taught classroom management. It was assumed that if you were a good teacher, you would already know how to handle children. But dealing with the behavior of children, just like any other activity, has to be learned. I thought I knew how to do it, but I had a lot to learn about managing a whole class of children. Fortunately, I had a great supervising teacher who knew I needed help and taught me some fundamental principles and methods that I have used my entire career with great success. As the years went by, I used the techniques that she had taught me and added many more that I learned from experience. [1]

Over the years, parents commented on how well the children listened and responded to me. Some wanted to know why, so I started

---

1 Immediately after college I took the Montessori training and the discipline principles my supervising teacher taught me coincided with those of Montessori's.

giving talks on behavior management to the parents at the school where I taught. A few years before I retired, I became aware that my approach was not exactly mainstream. One night, when my talk was finished, one of the parents sighed a big sigh as she choked back emotion and said, "I don't know what to do. *Everything* that you told us *not* to do we are doing with our son. We are doing it because all the professionals who work with him have told us this is what we are supposed to do. Where do I even begin to change this?"

Her son was autistic. In order to help him learn, the family had been attending therapy twice a week and had been working with the school district for years. Prior to coming to our school, he was enrolled in classes with other autistic children, and he had problems, but he was doing fine in my classroom. His behavior was excellent and he was motivated to learn. She told me that night that the psychologists wanted to put him on drugs.

When I asked her for examples of techniques they were using that I was against, she read down my entire list of points: they gave him lectures, they used stars and rewards, they never removed anything from him for bad behavior, they used tons of praise, they lied to him, they negotiated, they gave in, they bailed him out, and so on. The parents had been taught to avoid letting their son experience anything negative.

She knew that what she had been taught was wrong, but felt intimidated because all these directions came from the "experts." I really felt for her. I came away from the meeting thinking: Wow, it is really bad out there, much worse than I realized.

What really dismayed me, however, is that it is also worse than I realized in the Montessori world. Montessori trainers and teachers are also listening to what the so-called experts are recommending. And what they are recommending is in direct conflict with Montessori's approach. I have talked to teachers who work in Montessori schools where Montessori's words are ignored and ineffectual methods are being instituted. Incompetent approaches don't work and teachers are frustrated and unhappy. This saddens me immensely. The Montessori method is an integrated educational system with solid, proven principles that work. If those principles are compromised, the Montessori method will not work and the child will not thrive. Eventually the Montessori method will lose its uniqueness and dwindle away.

So I decided to write this book in order to explain why Montessori's approach to behavior management is the right one and to explain *my* approach, which is based on Montessori's. [2] My focus is on the child of normal development, not the child with exceptions, even though I have worked with special needs children. And I am talking about the child two to six years of age. (The basic principles still apply to older children, but the behavior issues are different.) While this book is for both teachers and parents, many discipline examples and situations are more heavily focused on the classroom. However, the appendices have discipline suggestions for both home and school.

---

2 If you are not already knowledgeable about the Montessori method, I refer you to *Montessori: A Modern Approach* by Paula Polk Lillard, *Maria Montessori: Her Life and Works* by E. M. Standing and/or my first book, *Montessori: Why It Matters for Your Child's Success and Happiness.*

CHAPTER 1
The Problem

Many years ago another Montessori teacher came to observe my classroom. At the end of the observation time I asked her if she had any questions, and her response was immediate, "Your children are so…they're so…well, they're so…calm!" She went on to tell me that she had a group of children who were a daily disruption to the entire class. They terrorized everyone by running around the room kicking and hitting the other children. She was never able to make any presentations without constant interruptions, and she said she really needed help in the area of discipline. I said, "Have you ever tried putting those children in a time-out chair?" "Oh no!" she stated emphatically, "Then everyone would know they were naughty."

Some years later we employed Montessori teachers in training who were told by their instructors not to put children in time-out.[1] Re-direction, or diverting the child's attention away from what he[2] is doing in order to change the misbehavior, was to be used instead, and teachers were never to draw attention to any child who misbehaved. Words like "no" and "don't" were to be avoided—the reason given was that those words were too negative and could damage a child's self-esteem. Teachers were told to refrain from using consequences and to either ignore misbehavior or negotiate with the child. I witnessed classes dissolving into chaos, with teachers following unruly

1 By this time I was a co-owner of a private Montessori school, as well as a teacher.

2 To avoid confusion, I generally refer to the child as "he" and adults as "she" except when I cite a specific incident where the child is female or the adult is male.

children around the room, endlessly re-directing them, reminding them to find work.

During the later years of my career, I noticed an increase in defiant and insolent children at our school.[3] Individual children were refusing to cooperate and were sassing their parents and teachers. They were becoming harder to handle, even violent. I witnessed children pushing over shelves, spitting on classmates, screaming obscenities at adults, throwing objects at people, shoving students into the wall, and then laughing when someone got hurt, and so on. A teacher, who worked at a nearby public school, reported that she had two concussions as a result of working with students with emotional and behavior disorders. Another teacher reported that students had ripped her classroom to shreds—overturning bookshelves and throwing furniture, breakables, and garbage around the room. When confronted, these unruly children would often place the blame elsewhere, claiming others had initiated the aggression.

These weren't only my observations. David Walsh, author of *No: Why Kids—of All Ages—Need to Hear It and Ways Parents Can Say It*, reports in his book:

> An Associated Press-Ispsos poll released in October 2005 found that nearly 70 percent of Americans said that children are ruder than they were twenty or thirty years ago. Millions watch the ABC program *Supernanny* to try to get their kids to behave civilly. Dr. Jean Twenge, social psychologist and author of *Generation Me*, released results of a study in April 2006 that showed that children today really are ruder than previous generations.[4]

Well-behaved children respect themselves, respect the rights of others, respect property, and obey the rules set up to enforce that respect. This isn't to say that they behave every single second. It is natural for children to test the limits, but in time, they learn why

---

3 In most cases, these were newly enrolled students, most of whom had been expelled from other schools for misbehavior. In other cases, the children were not being disciplined adequately either by the parents, the teachers, or both.
4 David Walsh, *No: Why Kids—of All Ages—Need to Hear It and Ways Parents Can Say It*, (New York: Simon & Schuster, 2007), p. 8.

those rules are necessary. At some point, they come to understand that if they disobey a rule about being careful with glass, it could break. They also become aware that there are things in the world that could hurt them, and they begin to pay attention to safety rules. So children will begin to obey these rules, even though not perfectly, as they will still make mistakes along the way. But sassing parents or running around the class abusing property and injuring other children on a regular basis does not constitute a well-behaved child. Montessori thought that patterns of disorderly and violent behavior in a child were "signs of emotional disturbance and suffering."[5] A child who "acts out" is not a self-assured, happy child, and he needs a caring, loving adult who has the courage to give him the help that he needs—discipline.

Discipline in regards to child behavior is often thought of as in-flicting "suffering, pain, or loss that serves as retribution" or "severe, rough, or disastrous treatment"[6] for the purpose of enforcing obedi-ence.[7] Control through the use of punishment is an incorrect defini-tion of discipline. An accurate definition is: "*training that corrects, molds, or perfects the mental faculties or moral behavior*"[8] and/or "*trains by instruction and practice, as in following rules or developing self-control.*"[9]

The proper purpose of discipline is not to make a child suffer or to inflict pain on him, but to teach him the difference between right and wrong, to keep him and others safe, to help him develop self-control, and to help him to think about actions and consequences. The end goal of discipline is for the child to ultimately achieve inde-pendence. Independence does not mean that the child is allowed to act on his whims, roam wild, and do whatever he wants whenever it pleases him. It means that the child can reason and act on his own thinking. The independent individual according to Montessori is one who "through his own efforts is able to perform the actions neces-

---

5 Maria Montessori, *The Absorbent Mind*, (New York: Dell Publishing, 1967), p. 253.
6 https://www.merriam-webster.com/dictionary/punishment
7 https://www.thefreedictionary.com/discipline
8 https://www.merriam-webster.com/dictionary/discipline
9 https://www.thefreedictionary.com/discipline

sary for his own comfort and development in life, conquers himself, and in so doing, multiplies his abilities and perfects himself as an individual." [10]

But discipline seems to have become a bad word. I observed parents sidestepping discipline with their children. They were not firm when they needed to be firm. When a child whined about something that he didn't want to do, the parent caved in to the child's demands. In the hallways when a child treated his parent with disrespect, the parent would stand timidly nearby, trying to talk his/her child into cooperating instead of correcting the rudeness.

More and more parents tried to shield their child from anything unpleasant. Teachers continuously received phone calls from parents worried that their child had encountered something uncomfortable, such as a falling out with a friend during recess, or parents who expressed undue concern when their child had to sit in time-out. When there was a conflict between the student and the teacher, the parents often sided with the child, even before talking to the teacher. Then, when the child didn't behave in class, they pronounced that it was the teacher's fault.

It wasn't always like this. Parents and teachers used to be on the same team. After a child complained about an incident in the classroom, the parents would first consult the teacher about what had happened, rather than automatically assume that their child's story was accurate. When a child misbehaved, it didn't matter if he didn't like his teacher—the parents still held the child responsible for his actions. Even when the teacher didn't do everything perfectly, the parents would insist that their child react with civility. [11] Adults didn't tolerate insolence and rudeness. Adults were in command of teaching behavior, and children knew it.

Teachers and parents have backed off from discipline. It is no coincidence that at the same time adults have become unassertive, children have become rude, violent, and disrespectful. Children need proper discipline, and they aren't getting it.

---

10 Maria Montessori, *The Montessori Method*, (New York: Schocken Books, 1965), p. 101.
11 By showing civility even when upset, the child learns mastery over himself. He learns how to act rationally, rather than impulsively.

In order to determine the proper educational methods for behavior, it is imperative that the facts about the child's nature be taken into account, because the wrong view of human nature leads to the wrong view of discipline. In the following pages I will explain the successful principles of discipline used in the Montessori classroom, which are based on Montessori's view of the child's nature, followed by an explanation of discipline practices based on her principles. And I will make the case that the reason the child isn't getting proper discipline is due to the false premises that are held about the child.

CHAPTER 2
Montessori's View of Discipline

In order for all the children in school to have an opportunity to learn, the students need discipline, otherwise there are constant interruptions as the teacher deals with behavior problems. Maria Montessori discovered that the key to good discipline is based on the nature of children. She recognized that children feel driven to learn about objective reality, and she provided an educational system (with a specific structure) conducive for them to do so. Then she observed that children achieve self-discipline through their work, not from a controlling adult, nor from an adult who allows children license to do whatever they feel like doing.

Self-discipline is "the ability to make yourself do things that should be done."[1] A child who is self-disciplined makes positive choices regarding his own behavior without prompts or commands from an adult. Montessori described a well-disciplined class as children who pursue knowledge independently while engaged in lively, productive activity.[2] "The greatest sign of success for a teacher... is to be able to say, 'The children are now working as if I did not exist.'"[3]

The first step for the child to achieve self-discipline is to learn how to concentrate. Montessori stated, "The first essential for the child's development is concentration. It lays the whole basis for his

---

1 https://www.merriam-webster.com/dictionary/self-discipline
2 Maria Montessori, *The Discovery of the Child*, (India: Kalakshetra Publications, 1966), p. 79.
3 Maria Montessori, *The Absorbent Mind*, (New York: Dell Publishing, 1967), p. 283.

character and social development."[4] However, concentration does not happen automatically; the child must learn how to do it: "He must find out how to concentrate, and for this he needs things to concentrate upon."[5] So she developed learning materials that meet the child's need for learning about reality. Since the child wants to learn about reality, he is naturally drawn to using these materials.

The purpose of the materials was to help the child understand aspects of the real world—identifying and classifying objects, discerning differences, cause and effect, and so on. The materials also promoted the development of independent problem-solving skills. The materials were self-correcting so that the child could tell for himself if he came to the correct conclusions. "[I]t is important to give him not only the means of education but also to supply him with indicators which tell him his mistakes."[6] These materials were presented to individual children when they were developmentally ready, and the children were left to practice without adult interference as long as they needed.

These materials were (and still are) key to the child's development of concentration. Because of the child's desire to learn about reality, the children were captivated and freely chose to work with them over and over. By working, the child learned to think more clearly and competently. He strengthened his reasoning powers. This resulted in the child's ability to become self-disciplined. The more competent the child became in his understanding of the facts of reality, the more self-control and confidence he developed, and the better behaved he became. She observed that even unruly children were transformed by their work. Once an engaging activity grabbed a child's attention, he learned to concentrate and a confident child began to emerge.

Montessori recognized that the child's self-esteem develops firsthand; it develops independently through his work: "Perfection and confidence must develop in the child from inner sources with which

---

4 Maria Montessori, *The Absorbent Mind*, (New York: Dell Publishing, 1967), p. 222.

5 Maria Montessori, *The Absorbent Mind*, (New York: Dell Publishing, 1967), p. 222.

6 Maria Montessori, *The Absorbent Mind*, (New York: Dell Publishing, 1967), p. 250.

the teacher has nothing to do."[7] "He constructs his mind step by step till it becomes possessed of memory, the power to understand, the ability to think."[8] The child's work[9] during childhood is to create the adult he will be when he grows up.

> [C]hildren construct their own characters, building up in themselves the qualities we admire. These do not spring up from our example or admonishments, but they result solely from a long and slow sequence of activities carried out by the child himself between the ages of three and six. At this time no one can 'teach' the qualities of which character is composed. The only thing we can do is put education on a scientific footing, so that children can work effectively, without being disturbed or impeded. Only later on is it possible to tackle the child's mind in a direct way, by means of reasoning and exhortation.[10]

Once children build their individual characters, they exhibit strong attraction toward the good. "They do not find it necessary to 'avoid evil.'"[11] And they even feel sorry for the child who misbehaves.[12]

In addition to learning how to concentrate and becoming self-confident by working with the Montessori materials, there is another very important element that must be present in order for self-discipline to develop among the children—the teacher. Her role in helping the children in her classroom achieve self-control is crucial. She has to be educated in the Montessori method so that she knows how

---

7 Maria Montessori, *The Absorbent Mind*, (New York: Dell Publishing, 1967), p. 274.

8 Maria Montessori, *The Absorbent Mind*, (New York: Dell Publishing, 1967), p. 27.

9 Maria Montessori, *The Absorbent Mind*, (New York: Dell Publishing, 1967), p. 167. What most people call play, Montessori calls work.

10 Maria Montessori, *The Absorbent Mind*, (New York: Dell Publishing, 1967), p. 208.

11 Maria Montessori, *The Absorbent Mind*, (New York: Dell Publishing, 1967), p. 241.

12 Maria Montessori, *The Absorbent Mind*, (New York: Dell Publishing, 1967), p. 229.

to properly prepare the environment and present the materials to the children. But this is not enough.

The children will not enter school and automatically become self-disciplined. (The notion that a child will spontaneously develop positively is a deterministic view that was introduced by "humanistic" psychology. See Chapter 5 for more on this topic.) As Montessori explained, the teacher needs to understand that "inner discipline is something to come, and not something already present. Our task is to show the way to discipline." [13] The teacher needs to help the child by maintaining order in the classroom and by actively correcting the children.

The first step for the teacher in the discipline process is to set limits. Paula Polk Lillard's book, *Montessori: A Modern Approach*, explains this and includes a point by Maria Montessori:

> [T]he child must be aided in developing a clear under-
> standing of good and evil. "The first idea that the child
> must acquire, in order to be actively disciplined, is that
> of the difference between good and evil." To achieve this
> distinction, the adult must set firm limits against de-
> structive and asocial actions. [14]

The rules that must be followed concern property respect, self-respect, and respect for others. Children may not damage or steal property, cause harm to themselves or their classmates, or interfere with anyone else's work. The children are also given lessons on proper social etiquette. Additional rules concern self-responsibility. If a child drops some work and makes a mess, he needs to clean it up. When a child is finished with his work, he is required to put it back on the shelf.

Once the rules have been established, it is up to the Montessori teacher to make sure the children follow the rules. The teacher needs to observe and supervise the class at all times, even when she is

---

13 Maria Montessori, *The Absorbent Mind*, (New York: Dell Publishing, 1967), pp. 263–264.
14 Paula Polk Lillard, *Montessori: A Modern Approach*, (New York: Schocken Books, 1972), p. 53.

presenting materials to individual children. Until the children learn how to work independently, Montessori thought that the teacher should "never turn her back on the class while she is dealing with a single child." [15] While observing the children, she must develop the ability to discern whether or not to intervene; she must be able to tell whether or not a child is genuinely working or wasting his time. "If the teacher cannot recognize the difference between pure impulse and the spontaneous energies which spring to life in a tranquilized spirit, then her action will bear no fruit." [16] If the teacher mistakenly stops productive activity, it could disrupt concentration and discourage good work. On the other hand, if she doesn't take measures to correct misbehavior, the learning atmosphere could fall apart.

Montessori put the responsibility of a well-run class directly upon the teacher. "[W]hen her class becomes undisciplined, the teacher sees in the disorder merely an indication of some error that she has made; she seeks this out and corrects it." [17] If she is faced with a class of unruly children, she needs to do more than simply show them work; she must be assertive and stop any negative activity. Montessori thought that useless or dangerous acts "must be suppressed, destroyed." [18] The teacher should determine how that should be done, which will depend on the circumstances, and then do it with no hesitation:

> When called on to direct a class of such children, the teacher may find herself in an agonizing situation if she is armed with no other weapon than the basic idea of offering the means of development and of letting them express themselves freely. The little hell that has begun to break loose in these children will drag to itself everything within reach, and the teacher, if she remains passive, will be overwhelmed by confusion and an almost

---

15 Maria Montessori, *The Absorbent Mind*, (New York: Dell Publishing, 1967), p. 271.
16 Maria Montessori, *The Absorbent Mind*, (New York: Dell Publishing, 1967), p. 264.
17 Maria Montessori, *The Absorbent Mind*, (New York: Dell Publishing, 1967), p. 285.
18 Maria Montessori, *The Montessori Method*, (New York: Schocken Books, 1964), p. 88.

unbelievable noise...She must call to them, wake them up, by her voice and thought. A vigorous and firm call is the only true act of kindness toward these little minds. Do not fear to destroy evil; it is only good that we must fear to destroy. Just as we must call a child's name before he can answer, so we must call the soul vigorously if we wish to awaken it. The teacher must remove her apparatus from the school and take away the principles from what she has learned; then she must face this question of the call, practically and alone. Only her intelligence can solve the problem, which will be different in every case. The teacher knows the fundamental symptoms and the certain remedies; she knows the theory of the treatment. All the rest depends on her...It is for her to judge whether it is better for her to raise her voice amid the general hubbub, or to whisper to a few children, so that the others become curious to hear, and peace is restored again.

A teacher of experience never has grave disorder in her class because, before she draws aside to leave the children free, she watches and directs them for some time, preparing them in a negative sense, that is to say, by eliminating their uncontrolled movements. [19]

Once the child has been given freedom, the teacher still carefully observes and monitors his development. The child isn't left completely free to do whatever he wishes whenever he wishes. Montessori viewed that as abandonment. [20]

Montessori had definite views on how children should behave and when they did misbehave, children were directly confronted [21] and firmly corrected. She did not think that children who misbehaved should be ignored; she was an advocate of solid, strong discipline:

---

19 Maria Montessori, *The Absorbent Mind*, (New York: Dell Publishing, 1967), pp. 268–269.
20 E. M. Standing, *The Montessori Method*, (California: The Academy Library Guild, 1962), p. 91.
21 In this context, confront does not mean starting a fight. It means naming the wrong doing to the child.

When the teachers were weary of my observations, they began to allow the children to do whatever they pleased. I saw children with their feet on the tables, or fingers in their noses, and no intervention was made to correct them. I saw others push their companions, and I saw on the faces of these an expression of violence, and not the slightest attention on the part of the teacher. Then I had to intervene to show with what absolute rigor it is necessary to hinder, and little by little suppress, all those things which we must not do so that the child may come to discern clearly between good and evil. [22]

In the Montessori classroom, freedom of movement is allowed, and because of it, children have the advantage of interacting socially. As the children move about the room, they have discussions with their friends and may choose to work with some classmates. They are allowed freedom to work out their social problems with each other, and all this provides a lot of opportunities to learn social skills. However, if a child disrespects property or the other students, Montessori advocated intervention:

If at this stage there is some child who persistently annoys the others, the most practical thing to do is interrupt him. It is true that we have said and repeated often enough, that when a child is absorbed in his work, one must refrain from interfering....[N]evertheless, the right technique now is just the opposite; it is to break the flow of the disturbing activity....[23]

Another discipline technique was used in Montessori's original schools with success—time-outs. A time-out is "a brief suspension of activity, break; a quiet period used especially as a disciplinary measure for children." [24] Time-outs can be used to calm a child or

---

22 Maria Montessori, *The Montessori Method*, New York: Schocken Books, 1964) pp. 92–93.
23 Maria Montessori, *The Absorbent Mind*, (New York: Dell Publishing, 1967), pp. 278–279.
24 https://www.merriam-webster.com/dictionary/time-out

to stop an unacceptable behavior. E. M. Standing, author of *Maria Montessori: Her Life and Work*, recalls:

> I once sent a questionnaire round to a number of long-established Montessori schools, and one of the questions in it was this: What use do you make of punishments? One directress wrote: "Work is its own reward. Punishments are rare; a troublesome child might be removed from her companions until she is ready to behave properly." Another said: "With younger children the greatest reward is to be able to pass on to a new stage in each subject. It is a punishment to a child not to be able to use the apparatus, but to sit still and do nothing." Another teacher (with twenty years of experience behind her) said: "If a warning does not suffice, the offender is separated from other children and made to sit beside the directress. [25] The lessons given by the directress to other children generally arouse interest and the child settles down to work. Either this or she becomes bored and returns to her place. This 'punishment' proves quite sufficient." [26]

Montessori wrote more fully about isolating a child:

> As far as punishments are concerned, we frequently found ourselves confronted with children who disturbed others, but who would not listen to our entreaties. We immediately had them examined by a physician, but very often they turned out to be normal. We then placed a little table in a corner of the room and, there isolating the child, we made him sit in an armchair where he could be seen by his companions and gave him all the objects he desires. This isolation always succeeded in calming the child. From his position he could see all of his companions, and their way of acting was an object les-

---

25 Even though the child is sitting next to an adult, this is still a time-out by definition.

26 E. M. Standing, *Maria Montessori: Her Life and Work*, (New York: New American Library, 1957), p. 44.

son in behavior more effective than words of his teacher could have been. Little by little he came to realize the advantages of being with the others and to desire to act as they did. In this way we imparted discipline to all the children who at first had seemed to us to be rebels...I do not know what happened within the souls of the isolated children, but certainly their conversions were always true and lasting. They became proud of their work and behavior, and they generally retained a tender affection for their teacher and for me. [27]

Instead of giving the child more work to punish misbehavior, she advocated withdrawing him from work and putting him in a position where he could learn proper behavior by observing the rest of the children. He also could observe the work all around him and see what he was missing. This was very effective. Isolation coupled with observation resulted in the misbehaving child discovering interesting work.

The children in Montessori's schools were permitted to work toward the ultimate goal of self-discipline by working with materials that gave them an understanding of the facts of reality. This process of developing self-discipline was managed by the teacher. The children were permitted to work without restrictions as long as they were engaged in purposeful activity, but if the behavior of any of the children became detrimental to themselves or someone else, the teacher was responsible for taking appropriate action. Montessori's method of discipline was groundbreaking because the children were not disciplined for the purpose of obedience to the teacher, as was traditionally done. Instead, they were disciplined for the purpose of developing independence.

Montessori's method of discipline was based on her view of human nature and what she thought children were capable of doing. Children are not raised the same way as puppies because there is a difference between the nature of humans and animals, and that difference is what enables humans to rise to a higher level of intelligence. Montessori thought that the difference was reason: "*A child*

---

27 Maria Montessori, *The Discovery of the Child*, (India: Kalakshetra Publications, 1966), p. 86.

starts with nothing and develops his reason, the specific characteristic of man." [28]

Reason is the faculty of the mind that uses logic to identify the facts of reality, to acquire knowledge, and apply it. Using reason, humans come to conclusions and make choices. It is reason, rather than physical strength, emotions, or "instincts" that humans rely on for their survival and advancement. Reason is critical not only for survival, it is also needed for moral behavior. When a child is faced with doing a moral or immoral act, he has to be able to think. He needs to consider the reasons why he should or shouldn't perform the action and the potential consequences of his choice. If he is able to consider all the facts logically, he then has the capability to make a wise choice.

Montessori thought that the child's education should focus on the development of his mind:

> The most important side of human development is the mental side. For man's movements have to be organized according to the guidance and dictation of his mental life. Intelligence is what distinguishes man from the animals, and the building up of his intelligence is the first thing to occur. Everything else waits upon this. [29]

The ability to reason is reliant upon the ability to make choices, upon free will. "Free will is the doctrine that the conduct of human beings expresses personal choice and is not simply determined by physical or divine forces." [30] Free will is "your mind's freedom to think or not, the only will you have, your only freedom, the choice that controls all the choices you make and determines your life and your character." [31]

There is no doubt that Montessori thought that humans have free will. She thought the child must build his reasoning powers with his

28 Maria Montessori, *The Secret of Childhood*, (New York: Ballantine Books, 1966), p. 61.
29 Maria Montessori, *The Absorbent Mind*, (New York: Dell Publishing, 1967), p. 72.
30 https://www.dictionary.com/browse/free-will
31 Ayn Rand, *For the New Intellectual*, (New York: New American Library, 1961), p. 127.

free will. "Free choice is one of the highest of all mental processes." [32] "A child chooses what helps him to construct himself." [33] The child self-creates; he can choose his own qualities, actions, and behaviors and is responsible for his own character.

Montessori thought that children were capable of acquiring the ability to reason, but identifying, integrating, and applying knowledge doesn't happen automatically. Children need to learn how to think accurately and efficiently. They also need discipline from the adult to assist in the process of learning how to reason. And learning how to reason is needed for moral behavior.

---

32 Maria Montessori, *The Absorbent Mind*, (New York: Dell Publishing, 1967), p. 271.
33 Maria Montessori, *The Absorbent Mind*, (New York: Dell Publishing, 1967), p. 223.

CHAPTER 3
Understanding the Child—2½ to 6 Years of Age

Appropriate discipline is reliant upon understanding the context of the child's mind. Inaccurate assumptions about what the child understands, feels, and/or what he is capable of doing lead to unrealistic expectations about how he should behave.

Adults can become very frustrated when a child is disciplined for a misbehavior and the child seems to understand that he shouldn't do it, but then keeps repeating that same misbehavior. Why does the child keep doing what he knows he shouldn't do? The explanation lies in the child's limited understanding of reality.

The child comes into the world knowing nothing about the world. To him, the world is exciting and new and learning all about it is serious business. The toddler can't resist touching everything in sight in order to learn what exists. He has a lot to figure out. Can a chair change into a dog? Can a man in a painting come alive? If a rock is thrown over a fence, will it still be a rock on the other side? If a spoon is dropped from a high chair, will it always go down?

The child is trying to grasp the nature of reality. He wants to know if it is what he perceives it to be, or is it something else? He wants to know if reality is stable or if it will change, so he tests it. One of my earliest memories was crawling around on the floor before I could walk and sticking my finger in an outlet to see what would happen. I found out! You would think after all my wailing and fretful tears that I wouldn't do it again, but children learn from repetition. Sometime later I was crawling around and saw another outlet. I wondered if the same thing would happen—finger in, electric shock, resulting in wails and tears again. The child is constantly testing reality, and that is how he learns about the world.

The child also tests adults over and over to see what will happen. David Walsh explains why children test adults: "Toddlers are not doing things parents don't want them to do just to be contrary. They are exploring this newly discovered difference between themselves and others."[1] He goes on to quote Alison Gopnik, a scientist and professor of psychology at Berkeley known for her work in cognitive and language development and causal learning. Gopnik co-authored *Scientist in the Crib*, which states:

> What makes the terrible twos so terrible is not that the babies do things you don't want them to do—one year olds are plenty good at that—but that they do things *because* you don't want them to…Toddlers are systematically testing the dimensions on which their desires and the desires of others may be in conflict…the child is the budding psychologist; we parents are the laboratory rats.[2]

Children test adults to see how far they can go and will keep an eye on their parents to see their reaction. "They are testing their limits, mapping the boundaries of their independence."[3] They know they are doing the wrong thing, but will do it anyway. Even when they know they should stop, they lack the ability to stop because the reasoning part of the brain, the pre-frontal cortex, is under construction and not fully working.[4]

The child wants to know what is permissible to do and what is never permissible to do. He knows that adults know more about the world and relies on them for guidance as to what is safe, dangerous,

---

1 David Walsh, *No: Why Kids—of All Ages—Need to Hear It and Ways Parents Can Say It*, (New York: Simon & Schuster, 2007), p. 123.
2 David Walsh, *No: Why Kids—of All Ages—Need to Hear It and Ways Parents Can Say It*, (New York: Simon & Schuster, 2007), pp. 123–124.
3 David Walsh, *No: Why Kids—of All Ages—Need to Hear It and Ways Parents Can Say It*, (New York: Simon & Schuster, 2007), p. 124.
4 David Walsh, *No: Why Kids—of All Ages—Need to Hear It and Ways Parents Can Say It*, (New York: Simon & Schuster, 2007), p. 124.

right, wrong, and so on. The child also judges by the reactions of adults just how serious certain actions can be. When I was five years old, I wondered how my father would react if I grabbed the steering wheel as he was driving the car and gave it a yank. I had never seen him so upset with me; his shocked and animated reaction was of titanic proportions, and I got the message—it wasn't just a dangerous thing to do, it was a *very* dangerous thing to do! And yet, sometime later, I wondered if I would get the same reaction if I did it again. I gave the steering wheel another yank and got the exact same response from my father. Note that before I tested my father by pulling on the steering wheel, I had some idea it would be an unsafe thing to do because I wanted to see how he would react, and his reaction confirmed and solidified in my mind the degree of the danger that I was inflicting. I never did it again.

Adults can misunderstand the child's intentions and mistakenly admonish him when he is going through some of his sensitive periods. A sensitive period is a time when the brain is at its peak for optimal learning of a specific skill without formal training. It is easily observable that children learn how to crawl, walk, and talk within the first three years of life without formal instruction, but most people are unaware that there are also sensitive periods for academics, concentration, social skills, order, and more. [5]

One of these periods that can be misinterpreted is the child's sensitivity to order, which peaks at age 2 to 2½. Children desire order, and not only do they desire it, they need it as they seek knowledge about reality. Maria Montessori discovered this sensitivity to order when a baby, about 6 months of age, cried when an umbrella was brought into the room and set on a table. The adults attempted to console the child, but nothing worked until the umbrella was removed from the room, whereupon the tantrum immediately ended. "The cause of her disturbance was the umbrella on the table. An object out of place had violently upset the little girl's pattern of memory as to where objects should be arranged." [6] When something unexpected happens, a child

---

5 For more information on sensitive periods see my first book, *Montessori: Why It Matters for Your Child's Success and Happiness*.
6 Maria Montessori, *The Secret of Childhood*, (New York: Ballantine Books, 1966), p. 50.

can become upset because he is trying to learn about the world, and change confuses him. As a result, the child may sulk, cry, or have a tantrum. Adults who do not understand why the child is distraught, may think he is being insolent and discipline him unnecessarily, when what the child needs is comfort.

Another period of development that is often misunderstood is the child's sensitive period for morality (age 2 to 6), which often results in "tattling." Children don't like it when rules are broken or someone does something the wrong way. It upsets their sense of order, so they come to the adult every time a rule is broken with a full, detailed report. The child then judges the seriousness of the infraction by the adult's response. Adults react with more concern when a child hurts another than they do when a child sticks out his tongue at someone else. The child is learning about right and wrong. He wants justice and stability and expects adults to maintain it. Adults, who do not understand this sensitive period, usually view "tattling" negatively and treat children who do it with disdain. This should not be done.

Whether a child needs to be reprimanded for lying depends on the nature of the lie. As a child tries to distinguish between reality and fantasy, he may try to work out something in his mind that he is trying to understand, so he tells a whopper. Or perhaps there is something that the child would really like to have in real life, so he talks about it as if it exists. Children who have imaginary friends, siblings, or pets fit into this category. If a child hasn't discovered yet that reality is unchangeable, he may wonder if something is true because someone says it is true, and then test this by lying. He might then continue to deny a wrongdoing, even when confronted by witnesses who saw him do it. Children will often lie just to see what will happen (will my words control reality?). Once the child can distinguish reality from fantasy, he may attempt manipulation which needs immediate correction. (Manipulation means to "change or manage skillfully by artful or unfair means so as to serve one's purpose."[7] Most children do not manipulate for a nefarious purpose: they are simply learning how to get what they want with certain people.)

---

7 https://www.merriam-webster.com/dictionary/manipulate

Children can be wrongly disciplined for using certain words when they do not have a full or even a correct understanding of those words. The child learns in sequential steps; he must first grasp simple concepts before more complex ones. For example, a four-year-old child does not have a complete understanding of the word "kill," because he does not comprehend the concept of death. If a child says he wants to kill someone, parents can get upset, when the child is just expressing anger towards that person. Or Thomas, age 4, called John a "baby," and then got in trouble for it. When Thomas was asked about it, he said John was upset and he was trying to get him to calm down. So he called him a baby. (Thomas thought that calling him a baby would calm him down.)

The child's limited understanding of concepts is the reason that explanations about what he should or shouldn't do is not enough to motivate him to stay safe or to behave. If an adult tells a child that cars can be dangerous, the concept of danger means something different to the adult from what it means to the child. The child's concept of danger goes something like this: "Mom said crossing the street without looking is dangerous. She said I could get hurt. I fell and scraped my knee and that really hurt and I cried. But it doesn't hurt anymore." Another reason why the child may not understand explanations as to why he should or shouldn't do something is his inability to think long-range. He can't think very far ahead. The child lives in the here and now. A child may be told to put on his coat because it is cold outside, but from the child's perspective, he isn't cold now so why should he put on his coat?

Teachers are often baffled when children continue to hit each other after it is explained to them repeatedly that hitting hurts other people. One reason why the hitting keeps happening is that the child doesn't understand cause and effect (if this happens, that will happen). He is starting to get the idea of cause and effect through his work with concrete objects: some break, some roll around, some bounce, some hurt when touched, and so on, but he needs lots of experience in order to predict what could happen if certain actions are performed on these objects. Cause and effect is even more difficult with people because they are more complex to predict, so the child tests them by hitting over and over. He also doesn't understand how to resolve conflict by talking because his language and reasoning ability is incomplete. Another aspect is that the child is not able to put himself in the shoes of another until age three, and some children can't do it until as late as age five. A child incapable of feeling empathy will not understand that hitting hurts other people.

People who think that children can reason like adults are making a massive mistake. The child cannot think like a grown-up because he has limited knowledge and abilities. The child is capable of learning how to reason within his own world. He can take two objects, count them, take two more objects, count them, and come up with the conclusion that 2+2=4. But he cannot foresee that if he runs out into the street he could get hit by a car and die. He hasn't experienced (or may not have witnessed) trauma; he has no idea what speed means or how to stop it; he has no idea that death is permanent; and so on. The child does not have the same context as an adult, and this needs to be understood in order to discipline properly.

CHAPTER 4
Discipline Practices Based on Montessori's Principles

Montessori's discipline method is unique because it focuses on the child's development of self-discipline. Since developing inner control is an ongoing process throughout childhood, the child needs additional guidance and correction as he grows up. The discipline in the original Montessori classrooms was successful because the teacher set limits and enforced those limits by using consequences. This chapter further explains discipline practices based on the principles of the role of the adult and the use of consequences.

The role of the adult. The teacher is the authority figure and has the responsibility for setting limits. Limits teach the child that reality is real and has a nature, that actions have consequences (as with a safety issue). Boundaries also help the child learn how to think and stop (or prevent) actions that could be detrimental to him or to someone else. When the limits are not followed, the adult has the authority to determine what discipline measures should be taken.

The adult knows more about the real world than the child, and for that reason, the adult is the child's agent for understanding reality. For example, the Montessori teacher is the link between the materials (reality) and the child. The teacher determines when a child is ready for a certain material, presents it to him, and then monitors his progress. And just as a teacher properly introduces materials to a child only when he is ready, she disciplines a child only when he is developmentally ready to learn certain behaviors. She properly guides him on the use of the materials just as she guides him with discipline. The child is not allowed to run wild without limits in any circumstance.

However, even though the teacher is the authority in the Montessori classroom, the discipline approach is not authoritarian. It is authoritative. An authoritative discipline approach provides clear expectations and consequences, but allows the child freedom within explained limits and adjusts discipline according to the child's maturity. The goal of the authoritative adult is to lead the child to self-discipline. This is not the same as the authoritarian approach, which also provides clear expectations and consequences, but without any explanations for those expectations. The authoritarian expects the child to cooperate because the adult said so; the goal is strict obedience rather than independence. The child raised by an authoritarian figure might behave, but he usually does so out of fear, rather than because of his own thinking.

Authoritative discipline can be likened to flying a kite.[1] Think of a kite as the child and the string as the gentle guiding hand of the adult. When the child exhibits maturity and responsibility, the string to the kite is let out as the child is given more freedom; but when the child misbehaves, the string is pulled back in as his freedom becomes more restricted. Since independence is developed over a continuum while the child is growing up, the adult is constantly adjusting the length of the string, pulling it in and letting it out, until the child reaches adulthood. Then the adult can completely let it go. The authoritarian, on the other hand, never lets the string out, not even when the child reaches maturity.

The approach that the adult uses when adjusting the kite will depend on the circumstances and the individual child. When the adult pulls the string back in, there may be times when the adult has to temporarily come across as an authoritarian and insist that the child do something that he refuses to do. This is especially important for a health issue. When a child refuses to take his medicine, the parent must insist he take it, and even enforce it, if the child continues to refuse. Insistence may also be needed for a child who doesn't yet understand rules that have been established for safety reasons or his long-range development, a disruptive or manipulative child who is unruly and defiant, or a child who has not yet learned how to focus.

1 Lena Wikramaratne, "Montessori Method," (lecture, Palo Alto, California, 1972–1973).

But this insistence from the adult is a temporary measure to help the child stop any negative activity or to get through phases in his life that have rules whose reasons he cannot yet comprehend.

The use of consequences. Consequences are the most effective type of discipline because children learn first-hand. Since young children cannot think long-range and do not fully understand cause and effect, consequences teach them that their actions have results, and they learn to think ahead. There are two types of consequences: natural and logical. A natural consequence happens without adult participation, whereas a logical consequence is instituted by the adult and imposed on the child.

Natural Consequences

There are many circumstances when the adult should refrain from intervening. When there is no danger or possibility of a serious outcome from a child's behavior, it is always best to let the child learn from the natural consequences of his choices and actions. Here is an example. After school at dismissal time, some children would refuse to put on their boots even though their parents told them it was cold outside. If it was safe enough (no chance of harm), some parents would let them walk out of the building without putting their boots on so they could feel the cold pavement beneath their bare feet. Parents reported that this was successful in motivating the children to put on their winter gear.

When Cassie was three years old, she went shopping with her mother. She wanted to bring a toy into the store, but her mother advised her not to do it, because she was afraid it might get lost. Cassie brought it into the store anyway and, sure enough, lost it. She went back into the store to look for it, but to no avail. Her mother did not purchase a replacement toy, so Cassie felt sad. Fast forward seven years to age ten when they went shopping with her younger sister. Her younger sister had a toy that she wanted to bring into the store. Cassie tried to talk her out of it: "Don't do it. Don't take it into the store. One time I did that and I lost it." When a child is allowed to experience the natural consequences of his actions, he learns from his mistake and remembers it longer.

Logical Consequences

When a natural consequence is dangerous, or if it doesn't work, the adult should set up logical consequences. The natural consequence for running across the street without looking for cars might be to get hit by a car. Since that could be perilous, logical consequences are set up instead. [2] A logical consequence should relate to what the child did. If the child runs out into the street without looking for cars, a logical consequence could be to ban the child from playing in the front yard until he develops awareness of the danger and more self-control. If a child runs in an area where running isn't allowed, a logical consequence would be to have him return to where he started and practice walking.

Logical consequences need to be tailored to each individual child according to his unique personality and set of circumstances. Any consequence given will depend on the age of the child, the reason he's doing what he is doing, household or classroom rules, the number of times he's broken the rule, the type of rule broken (for example, a safety issue needs to be dealt with quickly), and so on. A logical consequence may be to send him to his room, but if he loves going there, somewhere else should be chosen. The adult needs to find what works for *each individual* child. If possible, consequences need to relate to what the child did. If a child dawdles in the morning on a regular basis and doesn't get dressed, a logical consequence could be to take him to school in his pajamas. The child could even be asked, "Should I take you to school in your pajamas?" and it can be determined from the child's response what a good consequence might be. The child, if he is mature enough, can be invited to think of his own consequences, as long as the parent approves. Sometimes children think of very effective ones!

Once the consequences have been determined and set up, the adult should always be prepared to follow through with them. When

---

2 The idea of logical consequences came from Rudolf Dreikurs. Dreikurs was a psychiatrist, educator, and student and colleague of Alfred Alder. He developed Adler's system of individual psychology into a method for dealing with reprehensible behavior in children. Rudolf Dreikurs, *Children: the Challenge*, (New York: Plume, 1987).

parents back down in a discipline situation, children notice. The inconsistency creates confusion in the child's mind and makes the world seem unpredictable to him. The result is often a child who feels insecure and frightened. Some children eventually become angry and view their parent as weak. When a parent says to the child, "I love you, I'd do *anything* for you," how can the child believe it if the parent doesn't mean other things she says? The parent said she wouldn't let the child go to a movie because the child had misbehaved. Then she backed down, she gave in. Perhaps she will give in on other things. The child can conclude, "Maybe she lies when she says she'd do anything for me. She hasn't got the strength to do what she says she will do." Thus begins a cycle of the child's distrust in the adult.

Hands-on-hands technique. Some parents give instructions to a child, and then shrug their shoulders and do nothing when the child ignores them. If the child does not respond, the adult needs to follow through by taking appropriate action. It is usually best to give the child a heads up: "You can finish your picture and then we need to go home." But if the child doesn't make a move to leave when he is done, the adult needs to take him by the hand and walk him out to the car. When a child in school defiantly refuses to put his work away, the teacher needs to use the hands-on-hands technique. [3] She should put her hands on the child's hands, put the child's hands on the work, and walk with the child over to the shelf to put it away. After a few times of assisting the child in this manner, the child will comply on his own. When adults say what they mean and back it up with action, the child learns to pay attention to what is said to him.

Silence. Putting children "on silence" is effective when children are loud and unruly and won't calm down. Silence means not speaking. This is a useful method to use in the classroom when the children are too noisy, cruising around the room creating chaos. Or the children can be told to whisper—it is amazing how quickly they settle down and go back to work.

Surprise consequences. Surprise consequences can be used when the child knows the rules and has had enough reminders. One year, a class of students kept neglecting to push their chairs in, so

---

3 Wood, Paul, *How to Get Your Children to Do What You Want Them to Do*, (audio cassette), Pasadena, California: Cassette Works, 1977.

the teacher first explained the reasons why that needed to be done. Then she re-presented the lesson on pushing a chair in, and let them practice. Usually there was improvement in behavior after a re-presentation, but this time it fell flat—they continued to leave their chairs out. So one day the teacher and her assistants removed every chair that didn't get pushed in throughout the morning. By the time lunch time came around, all the chairs were gone and the children had to stand while eating lunch. The children were surprised and amused, but they got the point.

One winter night Bob and his family went to a holiday event. As they returned home, their two boys, aged four and five, were in the back seat fighting loudly. The parents told their sons to stop, but were ignored. So Bob told them to resolve their differences and stop fighting or they would have to walk the rest of the way home. The fighting continued. The car was stopped, the back door opened, and the boys stomped out, mumbling and grumbling under their breath as they began their walk home along the road. For those who may be concerned about danger, they were safe. They were on a snowy country road with essentially no traffic, and Bob drove slowly so that the car stayed right beside them as they trudged about three blocks home. In addition, it was cold, but not so cold that it would be unsafe. After that, car rides were quite peaceful.

Time-outs. When a child misbehaves and is told to take a time-out, he is sent to a spot where he is required to remain until he calms down. A time-out is a very effective type of consequence, because it stops the disruption. It also appeals to the child's mind. If he is sent to time-out at school, he has the opportunity to *think* about his actions while observing the proper behavior of the other children. If the child is at home and sent to his room, the alone-time gives him the chance to think about his misbehavior without distraction. Additionally, when a child is out of control or upset, a time-out helps him learn how to calm down and think more clearly. Adults help each other in the same manner when they suggest to a distraught friend to take a deep breath and count to ten and/or to take a break. Adults take time-outs, too. Composing oneself is an important life skill.

Time-outs are valuable for another reason. Parents often worry that their child won't learn anything at school if he is in the time-out chair, but as Montessori said, the first thing the child needs to learn is how to concentrate. A child won't learn how to concentrate by cruising around the room and disturbing the work of others. However, while the child is in time-out, he watches the academic activities of the other children, and in doing so, he can begin to learn how to focus.

Use of the word "no." Adults need to use the word "no" with children. Children need to learn that reality is what it is, it isn't negotiable, and it can't be changed. There are objective standards based on reality pertaining to morality and safety, and it doesn't matter whether they like it or not.

By the time a child is twelve to eighteen months of age, he should know the meaning of the word "no." He should understand that it means "stop." However, he most likely doesn't have enough self-control to always stop, and at that age there should be very few "no's," because it is very important that he be allowed to explore his world freely. But with his first "no" he learns that there are limits as to what he is permitted to do. It is important that he learn the meaning of this word because it is a step on the road to self-discipline.

Children need to learn self-control, and being told "no" goes a long way to helping them learn it. In the words of David Walsh, "No builds a foundation for self-discipline, self-respect and respect for others, integrity, perseverance, and a host of other character traits that lead to a happy productive life." [4]

At our school we had a six-year-old student who was choking other children—a very serious problem, so serious we thought we would have to dial 911 if it continued. We called the mother into the office and told her our plan. We wanted to isolate her child. We would give him his own table for three months. He was to stay there to do his work and couldn't get up without permission. The mother was upset because she thought he would conclude he was naughty and it would damage his self-esteem. She thought the other kids wouldn't like him (as if they liked him now). We told her that the safety of the children was our top priority, so either he would need to be isolated or he would have to leave the school. She loved Montessori, so she consented to the plan.

4 David Walsh, *No: Why Kids—of All Ages—Need to Hear It and Ways Parents Can Say It*, (New York: Free Press, 2007), p .3.

Toward the end of the three months when it was time to give him his freedom again, he asked his mother, "Are my three months almost over?"

"Yes," she said.

He proceeded to get upset.

"What's wrong?" his mom asked. "Why are you upset?"

"When I am working at my table, I don't hurt anybody. I don't want to leave my table."

Telling him "no" gave him the boundaries he needed to start controlling himself. A child needs to hear the word "no" said to him so that he can say it to himself later.[5]

---

5 William Sears, "How to Say No," Ask Dr. Sears, https://www.askdrsears.com/topics/parenting/discipline-behavior/how-to-say-no

CHAPTER 5
Alternate Discipline Practices

In order to achieve good self-discipline, the child needs two things: he needs to develop his reasoning skills by acquiring knowledge about reality and he needs discipline from the adult. Unfortunately, most educational systems do not center around cognitive development. Cognitive development is ignored due to philosophical ideas that have gained traction in our culture. Chief among these ideas detrimental to discipline is determinism.

Determinism is the theory that every aspect of a human being's life and character is the result of factors beyond his control.[1] Determinists think that humans do not have free will and do not have control over their lives. One view of this theory is that the child is determined by his environment, which includes family, society, school, relationships with others, and so on. Montessori strongly disagreed: "*Environment* is undoubtedly a *secondary* factor in the phenomena of life; it can modify in that it can help or hinder, but it can never *create*."[2] Who or what creates the child then, according to Montessori? The child himself. The determinist view of human nature, in direct conflict with Montessori's view that humans can reason, has led to views on discipline that have had a major impact on children's behavior.

---

1 For a validation of the concept of free will and its basis in reason see *The Illusion of Determinism, Why Free Will is Real and Causal* by Edwin A. Locke.
2 Maria Montessori, *The Montessori Method*, (New York: Schocken Books, 1964), p. 105.

Progressive Education

The dominant educational philosophy in our country is progressive education. The premise of progressive education is that the child's social life forms the basis for his development and provides the background for his work and accomplishments. Therefore, the school should revolve around social activities rather than learning objective facts.[3] The teacher is not an authority; the authority is shared by all the students. Therefore, discipline should not come directly from her, nor should she control the educational process.[4]

Progressive education is based on the ideas of John Dewey (1849–1952), a social determinist who did not believe in free will and thought that the individual is formed by his relationships with others[5] and that social institutions "are a means of creating individuals."[6] Unlike Montessori who thought that the starting point for a child's development was concentration, he thought the starting point was the child's social life: "I believe that the social life of the child is the basis of concentration, or correlation, in all his training or growth."[7] Unless there was some social benefit, he viewed the individual pursuit of knowledge as a negative objective and even discouraged it. He did not think that objective truth exists: "Quest for certainty that is universal, applying to everything, is a compensatory perversion."[8] Instead, he thought that truth is whatever the group believes.[9]

---

3 John Dewey, "My Pedagogic Creed," School Journal vol. 54 (January 1897), pp. 77–80.
4 John Dewey, "My Pedagogic Creed," School Journal vol. 54 (January 1897), pp. 77–80.
5 John Dewey, "Human Nature and Conduct," https://freeditorial.com/en/books/human-nature-and-conduct and "Democracy and Education," https://archive.org/details/democracyandeduc00deweuoft/page/n159, p. 143.
6 John Dewey, "Reconstruction in Philosophy," https://freeditorial.com/en/books/reconstruction-in-philosophy.
7 John Dewey, "My Pedagogic Creed," School Journal vol. 54 (January 1897), pp. 77–80.
8 John Dewey, The Quest for Certainty (New York: G.P. Putnam's Sons, 1960), p. 228.
9 https://en.wikipedia.org/wiki/Pragmatic_theory_of_truth Dewey stated in Logic: The Theory of Inquiry that the best definition of truth is that by Peirce: "The opinion which is fated to be ultimately agreed to by all who investigate is what we mean by the truth, and the object represented in this opinion is the real. [CP

Dewey's view that education should be centered around social development instead of cognitive development has come to be accepted, and you will find the progressive educational approach in most schools today, both public and private.

Peer pressure. Because progressive education is a socially based system, peer pressure is often used as a disciplinary measure. Peer pressure is the process whereby a group of people attempt to coerce others to conform to some standard or ideology. Those pressured feel that they must conform in order to be liked or respected. It can be done by one group pressuring outside individuals or by making a group or a few members responsible for what each individual within the group does. In the realm of discipline, rather than the adult managing misbehavior, the children are expected to take control and manage it themselves. Teachers in progressive schools can rely on the well-behaved children to monitor and pressure the rest of the students to work and behave. Some students are even told explicitly that they are responsible for the actions of the students in their group. [10]

In the Montessori classroom, peer pressure is not an issue because the Montessori method is cognitively based, rather than socially based. Each child progresses academically at his own rate, instead of with a group, and is treated as an individual; there is no expectation that each child should be the same as the rest of the students. Montessori children do not feel the need to conform to the dictates of others in order to be accepted. Consequently, peer pressure is not used for behavior management. The rules are objectively defined and then enforced by the teacher.

Progressive education actually creates climates that are conducive for misbehavior to flourish. The premise that good child development is reliant upon social acceptance, rather than cognitive development, is the root of the problem. First, since learning is not given priority, a child can feel that he is a failure at learning; he can conclude that something is wrong with him, and feel stupid, and then act out in class when the teacher asks him to answer a question about the subject matter. Secondly, children in these educational settings can get the message that in order to be a worthwhile person, they must be accepted

---

5.407]. (Dewey, 343 n).

10 The use of peer pressure can vary from school to school and teacher to teacher.

and liked by others. If they accept that message, their behavior will reflect the standards of the group, even if those standards are wrong.

Behaviorism

The use of rewards and punishments to change behavior is advocated by behaviorism, a view that behavior is determined by stimuli in the environment. It is based on the work of researchers who discovered that positive or negative reinforcement could shape the behavior of animals and concluded that this also applied to the behavior of humans. B. F. Skinner (1904–1990), a behaviorist and psychologist who considered free will to be an illusion, developed a procedure called behavior modification, a method that punishes negative behaviors in order to get them to end and rewards positive behaviors so that they will continue.

Montessori opposed using rewards, punishments, praise, and/or criticism as a means to motivate a child to do well. "To tell a person he is clever or clumsy, bright, stupid, good or bad, is a form of betrayal. The child must see for himself what he can do..." [11] She thought the child should develop the ability to evaluate himself and his behavior should be internally motivated, rather than dependent on the appraisal of others. Plus, the child's accomplishments with his work provides him with all the "reward" he needs.

Behavior modification became widely used in 1968, and, although it is not used as much today, it is still influential. Behaviorism has led to or sustained the use of such practices as spanking, bribes and rewards, praise, and ignoring misbehavior.

Spanking. Spanking is the attempt to make the child suffer physically for what he did, and for that reason, it is punitive. It is often an illogical consequence—in most cases it has no relation to what the child did. For example, Conner was told to be careful with the vacuum, because if he keeps shoving it into the wall, he could break the vacuum or crack the wall. Conner continued to do it so the adult spanked him. The logical consequence would have been to ban him from using the vacuum for a period of time. Inflicting pain does not

---

11 Maria Montessori, *The Absorbent Mind*, (New York: Dell Publishing, 1967), p. 250.

result in the child thinking about his wrongdoing while he is being spanked—he just focuses on the pain. In addition, spanking teaches the child nothing about self-control. It is hypocritical to try to teach a child to refrain from hitting other children when he is angry, when the adult turns around and hits the child when the adult is angry. But the worst consequence of spanking is that the child can come to fear the adult.

Bribes and rewards. Eric, age five, was in constant trouble in school for hitting other children. When disciplined for it, he didn't seem to care. Finally one day, when put in a chair for hitting again, he sat and cried with his head in his hands. The staff thought they had finally made a break-through. But they were sorely disappointed when he choked out these words in between his sobs: "Now that I've had to sit in the chair, I won't get to see a movie when I go home." Unfortunately, this is what happens when a child is offered a reward for good behavior—he focuses on the reward rather than his actions. Eric wasn't thinking about the fact that he had hurt someone by hitting him. He was thinking about the movie.

When parents offer rewards, they assume the responsibility for the child's behavior. The parent sits in the driver's seat, deciding when the child's behavior is good enough, discouraging the child from judging for himself. The parent has the power and grants the child a prize if he cooperates. So the child's focus shifts to the envisioned prize. He thinks, in essence, "What will I get?" rather than, "How should I behave?"

One of the worst messages that a child can take away from this type of discipline is the expectation that he will get something from others in return for acceptable behavior: "What are you going to give me?" This thought process can turn the child into a manipulator as he gets older: "I won't behave unless I get something." If the child likes external rewards, then he may continue to hit once in a while so that adults will give him a reward when he doesn't hit. He may feel that the world revolves around him, and that what happened to the other child doesn't matter.

Rewards also prevent the child from learning cause and effect. For example: Oliver is having a temper tantrum because he wants to be first in line. The parent offers him a piece of candy if he stops crying.

Oliver stops, eats the candy, but has another tantrum later hoping to get more candy. He didn't feel the correct effect of his behavior; he didn't learn that tantrums will not gain him anything. Quite the opposite. Had the bribe not been offered, the child would have learned to calm himself on his own and that he gets nothing for throwing a fit.

Behavior improves gradually as a child figures out the ways of the world and how they relate to him. It is not an overnight change—it takes time and conscious effort. Another problem with rewards is that they demand an immediate transformation, and even when the child is improving, he may get the message that he isn't good enough because he didn't get a reward. So he may feel like a failure even though he is making progress.

If the parent thinks her child needs a concrete way to see his development so that the child can evaluate his progress for himself, setting up a chart to record his behavior may be acceptable in some cases. However, the adult should not place any stars on the chart— the child should do that; he should be evaluating his own behavior and deciding if he should give himself the star. At the same time, the parent should monitor this process and not allow the child to lie or fake reality by letting him have a star if he hasn't really earned it. If the child reaches his goal of a certain number of stars, the parent can say, "Doesn't it feel good? Would you like to celebrate in some way? What would you like to do?" This puts the ball in the child's court and gives him a sense of control over his life.

Rewards have their place, but shouldn't be used as a form of discipline. Rewards used as a way to change unacceptable behavior are bribes, not actual rewards. Real rewards are used to celebrate accomplishments and are secondary to the inner satisfaction one feels from those accomplishments. Furthermore, rewards are not given for every little triumph, but rather are used for long-range achievements. When a child is given rewards for his every success, he becomes used to being the center of attention and continues to expect it from others as he grows up. And he has been denied the pride that he could have felt had he focused on his accomplishments, rather than the rewards.

Praise. Some people try to manage a child's behavior through praise. They use praise as a means to get a child to continue to behave in a certain way or to gain a child's cooperation. Their objective is to raise the child's self-esteem so that he will behave or continue to behave. The danger of using praise to manage behavior is that the child becomes less likely to evaluate himself, and he learns that his self-worth is reliant on what others think of him. Dependency on others does not lead to good behavior, especially when peer pressure to do something wrong becomes an issue.

A friend of mine couldn't understand why his son got into so much trouble: "But we gave him plenty of praise!" People think that if you praise a naughty child, you will spare the child looking at his negative characteristics. If he isn't aware of them, he will feel good about himself. But faking reality does not help the child. How will he know to correct himself when he hasn't been told what he needs to correct? Praise needs to be based on the facts of reality, and feedback to the child needs to help him, not hinder him—and meaningless messages do not give anyone concrete proof that they are okay.

Instead of over-praising the child, encourage him to evaluate himself by giving him specific feedback so that the child knows where to focus his attention next time. "I see that you are learning how to clean. I don't see any dirt on the floor," rather than, "Good job!" Or, "You noticed your friend was thirsty and offered him some water," rather than, "You are so smart."

Some people think that a child should never be praised, but there are times when the adult needs to acknowledge the child's accomplishments. A child who works and works to achieve a certain goal will want recognition for it. Dr. Montessori stated, "This, however, is the moment in which the child has the greatest need of [the teacher's] authority. When a child has accomplished something...he runs to the teacher and asks her to say if it is all right....After he has done the work, he wants his teachers' approval....The teacher must respond with a word of approval, encouraging him with a smile...." [12]

Praise can be given spontaneously to express one's joy at what the child has accomplished, or to express love for that child, but not as a means of convincing him that he is a worthwhile person in order to manage his behavior. He learns that he is worthwhile through his

12 Maria Montessori, *The Absorbent Mind*, (New York: Dell Publishing, 1967), p. 274.

own competency, not from praise. And it is competency that leads to good behavior.

Ignoring misbehavior. Giving a child attention for a behavior is viewed by behaviorists as reinforcing it, even if it is negative attention. Hence, ignoring misbehavior is advocated.

Ignoring a mild misbehavior such as whining is fine (providing the child is told that whining is unacceptable and he will be ignored when he does it), but it is not okay to ignore major acts of misbehavior. Non-confrontation does not give the child any information about his behavior, so he continues to misbehave.

Picture this actual event. The Montessori classroom is filled with four-foot high, free standing shelves full of materials, many of which are breakable. Joseph, age five, looked around to see if anybody was watching, then picked a shelf and walked on top of it. This was clearly dangerous. If he fell to the floor, he could seriously injure himself; if a shelf fell over, any child in its way could get hurt. The head teacher was a good teacher and a good disciplinarian generally, but she didn't know how to handle children with aggressive, hazardous behaviors. She had heard about the theory that children like this should be ignored and so she ignored him. Not only did his behavior not get any better, it got worse. He jumped from shelf to shelf, and then stomped across each one, causing them to wobble. He grinned from ear to ear while the rest of the children huddled together in groups and watched him from afar with anxiety in their eyes. From the child's point of view, it must be a pretty scary situation when an adult cannot or does not stop something unsafe.

Humanistic Psychology

In the later-half of the twentieth century, a hands-off approach to managing behavior emerged. The belief was that if a child is allowed unlimited freedom, he will eventually reveal his true self, and his creative side will spring forth. This approach has its source in humanistic psychology, which maintained that it supported the idea of free will, as opposed to behaviorism, but it actually advocated for another form of determinism, because it held the idea that the child already has a "true self." The child doesn't construct it, it is already there. All the child has to do is reveal it by "blooming," but in order for that revelation to happen, certain conditions are needed.[13]

One of the founders of humanistic psychology was Carl Rogers (1907–1987) who thought that children can develop properly without adult assistance. He thought that education should be directed by the child and that the child should be allowed to develop spontaneously without any interference from the teacher, who should not be regarded as an expert.[14] He strongly endorsed A. S. Neill's school, Summerhill, which was created in 1921 in Suffolk, England. At Summerhill, all the children had an equal say in how it was managed. The students voted on the rules and were even allowed to choose whether to attend classes.[15] In 1960, Neill wrote a book, *Summerhill*, explaining the philosophy and approach used at the school. Rogers wrote a recommendation, published on the back cover of the book itself, lauding the school's rejection of authority, assignments, examinations, and discipline. Summerhill, he held, exemplified the Rogerian, non-interventionist view that "when children are given a responsible freedom, in a climate of understanding and non-possessive love, they choose with wisdom, learn with alacrity, and develop genuinely social attitudes."[16]

Montessori thought children needed boundaries and discipline from the teacher, and for those reasons humanists thought that her method was too controlling. Eda LeShan, author of *The Conspiracy Against Childhood*, criticized the Montessori method because she thought that the children were too well-behaved. She found fault because, she said, the majority of the children were not rebellious and restless; they were polite, instead of yelling at one another. She claimed that the vitality of the children had been repressed.[17]

---

13 Saul McLeod, "Carl Rogers," in Simply Psychology, updated 2014 https://www.simplypsychology.org/carl-rogers.html

14 https://en.wikipedia.org/wiki/Carl_Rogers. Thomas Gordon, the developer of Parent Effectiveness Training, was once a student of Carl Rogers and later a colleague.

15 A.S. Neill, *Summerhill*, (New York: Hart Publishing, 1960), pp. 4, 5, 8, 20.

16 Carl Rogers, Review on book cover, *Summerhill*, by A.S. Neill, Hart Publishing, 1960.

17 Eda J. LeShan, *The Conspiracy Against Childhood*, (New York: Atheneum, 1968), pp. 73–78.

Permissiveness. Permissiveness is the idea that children should have unlimited freedom—they should be set free to do as they like whenever they like. With permissive parenting there are few, if any, rules or guidance, and when the children misbehave, the parents usually have an excuse such as, "Kids will be kids." Children raised with this approach typically operate on chance and whim instead of reason, and they lack self-control.

Positive Discipline

An increasingly popular approach to discipline is positive discipline, a socially based approach to managing behavior that has its roots in the ideas of John Dewey. Its adherents think that the adult should be non-authoritarian and indirect and institute continuous re-direction instead of consequences. Collaboration and/or meetings are advocated where everyone has a say or a vote in the rules. The approach is group-oriented.

Some of the main people whose ideas have directly or indirectly contributed to positive discipline are Rudolph Dreikurs (1897–1972),[18] author of *Children: the Challenge*; Alphie Kohn,[19] author of *Punished by Rewards*; and Jane Nelsen,[20] author of *Positive Discipline*. While all three have made valuable contributions in dealing with children,[21] they also have mixed premises and it is the wrong premises which have negatively affected the development of attitudes toward discipline.

Role of the adult. Contrary to the Montessori approach, positive discipline does not view the adult as an authority figure. Rudolf Dreikurs thinks adults should completely relinquish their authority:

> In order to understand the power struggle fully and to develop techniques for dealing with it, we must re-evaluate our position as parents. We must become very much

18 Rudolf Dreikurs was influenced by Immanuel Kant (1724–1804), who held that there is no absolute truth, a view with which Dreikurs concurred.
19 Alphie Kohn is a progressive in education.
20 Jane Nelsen was influenced by Dreikurs.
21 Such as communicating with children respectfully.

aware of our new role as leaders and give up completely our ideas of authority. We simply do not have authority over our children. [22]

The notion that adults should completely give up their authority is worse than false; it is totally irresponsible and unethical. As one example, if given unlimited freedom, there would be some children who would eat candy and sugar non-stop instead of healthy food. Allowing a child to eat nothing but candy would be child neglect. Children are not capable of deciding everything themselves. If they were capable, they would have no need to be raised or educated by an adult. Children do not have the long-range understanding about what they need to learn and do in order to develop a moral code and develop the qualities required for their long range well-being and happiness. Children *need* adults. Adults have the knowledge to correct, protect, and keep children safe. Children are reliant upon adults for *their very survival!*

When a child is misbehaving and the adult does not take charge, the child can manipulate the adult. Often the adult has no idea what is going on and unknowingly keeps catering to the child. If the child learns that he can get away with stalling, he will. If he doesn't have to get dressed in the morning, he won't. If he fakes being sick so that he can be home with Mom and the lie works, he'll try it again. One time I asked a three-year-old why he misbehaved with his mother. "Because I get what I want," he replied.

Peer Pressure. Peer pressure, as an approach to discipline, has its beginnings in progressive education, and is practiced in positive discipline as a means of behavior management. It is practiced in classroom meetings where children are allowed to meddle in the conduct of their classmates. (See the section on classroom meetings later in this chapter.) It is also promoted by Dreikurs who, unlike Montessori, does not support dealing with each child as an individual when behavior issues arise.

Dreikurs thinks that disciplining children on an individual basis when they misbehave promotes competition among the children for

---

22 Rudolf Dreikurs, *Children: the Challenge*, (New York: Plume, 1987), p. 152.

parental approval. The child who is in trouble gets pushed down and the other well-behaved child elevated. So each child compares himself to his siblings and tries to be better to get attention. The child's interest then centers upon himself and where he stands with his parents, rather than "contributing to the common welfare." Therefore, Dreikurs thinks that the parent should put all the children in a group and treat them as a unit, making the group responsible for what each member does.[23]

Disciplining children on an individual basis is not what promotes competition among siblings for parental attention. Dreikurs assumes that when one sibling is in trouble, the other one feels superior, but that isn't necessarily true. Sometimes one sibling comes to the other's defense or learns from the discipline: "Boy, I'm not going to make *that* mistake!" Children want love from their parents and are aware of the attention that their siblings receive. They do not understand that loving one child does not mean the parent loves another child any less. That understanding comes with maturity. So some children, for that and other reasons, will compete to gain that attention.

Is it unfair to make the innocent pay for something they didn't do? Dreikurs doesn't think so, but it is unfair because it removes responsibility from the wrongdoer. Dreikurs reasons that if we make children responsible as a group for what each member does, they will have no desire to misbehave. I disagree. What about when one sibling gets mad at another and misbehaves in order to get them all in trouble? Or what about the child who misbehaves in a group because he knows he won't be held responsible, that other people will be held responsible? Some children conclude: why should I be good when I am punished anyway?

Dreikurs says treating all children as a unit removes competition and moral judgement.[24] He thinks these are desirable outcomes. But in fact, moral judgment will still occur if good behavior is the goal, and treating the children as one unit would create power struggles

23 Rudolf Dreikurs, *Children: the Challenge*, (New York: Plume, 1987), pp. 257–259.
24 Rudolf Dreikurs, *Children: the Challenge*, (New York: Plume, 1987), pp. 257–259.

among the siblings where they try to pressure each other to either behave or misbehave.

Another result of treating children as a unit is that all the children get punished for what one child does. In a school setting the entire class gets punished. What kind of a social atmosphere does this create? Not a benevolent one. The children all start pointing fingers at who is to blame for their unjust predicament. If the goal is to create an environment where all the children feel accepted by each other and that each is a significant contributor to the community, this won't do it. Instead of fostering a community, it creates an atmosphere of distrust and division. To make others responsible for another individual's behavior is reprehensible.

Reason for misbehavior. Positive discipline claims that a child's behavior is determined by his perception of his relationships with others. It holds that if a child feels a sense of connection to the community, family, and school, he is less likely to misbehave. Rudolph Dreikurs "suggested that human misbehavior is the result of feeling a lack of belonging to one's social group." [25] Jane Nelsen agrees and states that "the primary goal of all human beings is to feel a sense of belonging and significance." [26] If a child does not feel that he belongs, he will misbehave:

> Behavior is determined within a social context. Children make decisions about themselves and how to behave, based on how they see themselves in relationship to others and how they think others feel about them. [27] ... The primary goal is to belong. [28] ... So, how do you know when a behavior is misbehavior? The key is discouragement. Children who feel discouraged about their ability to belong are more likely to misbehave. [29] ... A misbe-

25 Rudolf Dreikurs, https://en.wikipedia.org/wiki/Rudolf_Dreikurs and Children: the Challenge, (New York: Plume, 1987).
26 Jane Nelsen, *Positive Discipline*, (New York: Ballantine Books, 1987), pp. 33–34.
26 Jane Nelsen, *Positive Discipline*, (New York: Ballantine Books, 1987), p. 33.
27 Jane Nelsen, *Positive Discipline*, (New York: Ballantine Books, 1987), p. 33.
29 Jane Nelsen, *Positive Discipline for Preschoolers*, (New York: Crown Publishing Group, 2007), p. 142.

> having child is trying to tell us "I don't feel I belong or
> have significance, and I have a mistaken belief about
> how to achieve it." [30] ... If you remember that behind the
> misbehavior is a child who just wants to belong and is
> confused or unskilled about how to accomplish that goal
> in a socially useful way.[31]

The idea that children misbehave because they don't feel like they belong to their social group is a wrong premise and a considerable mistake. Groups of children, good buddies, can create havoc together and the leaders of those groups can act emboldened because they have followers. Loners, or even children who are not well liked, can be very well behaved. Loving, caring parents might be faced with raising a disruptive, ill-mannered child. Love and acceptance aren't enough to determine behavior.

The child's behavior is based on the conclusions he draws from his knowledge and the choices he makes because of those conclusions; it is based on his ability to reason. A child may understand that doing something is wrong, but not understand all the ramifications of that wrongdoing. He does not have enough conceptual knowledge to understand all the reasons why he is being told to stop doing what he wants to do. He does not entirely grasp logic. The child is still learning about what exists, and that is his primary goal—to learn about reality, not to belong.

But regardless of the reasons for a child's misbehavior, peer conformity should not be encouraged. It sets the stage for compliance instead of independence. By accepting the premise that a child should feel like he belongs to a group in order to act properly, adults are putting the child in a position where he is expected to submit to the standards of his peers. His peers may or may not have proper standards for behavior, especially if the adults have withdrawn as authority figures. If the child gets the message that it is more important to be liked than to learn, he will seek out their approval in order to be liked. If a group has the wrong standards for behavior and its participants decide to do something wrong, then, ironically, the inse-

---

30 Jane Nelsen, *Positive Discipline*, (New York: Ballantine Books, 1987), p. 34.
31 Jane Nelsen, *Positive Discipline*, (New York: Ballantine Books, 1987), p. 35.

cure child also misbehaves, not because he doesn't feel accepted, but because of his desire to be accepted. The cause of his misbehavior in this instance is dependency.

Seeking social acceptance, rather than the facts of reality, can have a lasting negative impact on a child's life. Because he does not develop his own mind independently, he relies on what other people say is true. Since different people say different things, his mind swings from one opinion to another based on what he hears. He is so dependent on other people that he has no authentic thoughts or convictions of his own, sometimes not even his own likes and dislikes. His priority in life is to be approved by others. Seeking approval is so prevalent that he can become very meek and obedient (a people pleaser), become obsessed with the desire to be admired, and/or end up trying to control others.

Peer pressure to conform in school sets the child up to be a second-hander as an adult. The basis of reality for the second-hander becomes the group instead of the real world because he learned to look to others for the truth. "A [second-hander] is one who regards the consciousness of other men as superior to his own and to the facts of reality. It is to a [second-hander] that the moral appraisal of himself by others is a primary concern which supersedes truth, facts, reason, logic." [32]

As an adult he is psychologically weak. He is so fearful of social rejection that he is unable to oppose irrationality or to stand up for what is right, if he even knows what is right. If he becomes a parent and needs to discipline his child, he lacks confidence. Not only does he lack the moral certainty that he is disciplining correctly and for the right reasons, he is afraid of being rebuffed by his own child.

Time-outs. Positive discipline advocates are opposed to sending children to time-outs. Jane Nelsen, one of the main proponents of positive discipline, states: "It is unlikely that children who are sent to time-out are thinking about what they did. It is more likely that they are thinking about what you did and how disrespectful and unfair you are." [33] Instead, Nelsen advocates positive time-out areas. Positive time-out areas are places where children are given a choice to go in

---

32 Ayn Rand, *The Virtue of Selfishness*, "The Argument from Intimidation," (New York: Penguin Books, 1964), p. 165.
33 Jane Nelsen, *Positive Discipline*, (New York: Ballantine Books, 1987), p. 129.

order to calm down, so that the conflict can be resolved later.[34] In the positive time-out area, the child can do something enjoyable, such as play with toys, read, rest, or listen to music. The purpose of positive time-outs is to help children feel better so they can think rationally, not to make them feel worse or to "pay" for what they have done. Nelsen holds that solutions should not be focused on until everyone has calmed down. [35]

Montessori noted that children learn proper behavior from observing the well-behaved children, so it is doubtful that the children who are sent to time-outs don't think about what they did. Additionally, time-outs are not disrespectful or unfair. They are not done by putting a child up in front of the room with a dunce hat on so that the other children can laugh at him. And they are not done in a way to make the child suffer physically. The child is simply told to sit in one place so that he may no longer disrupt the class. If a child does think that the adult is disrespectful and unfair, are we to refrain from correcting a child because of that? Children want to do what they want to do and don't like to be stopped, but with maturity, they understand why they were corrected.

It is true that calming down is important in order to think rationally, but the purpose of a time-out is not to make them "pay" for what they have done. It *does* give the child time to calm down and it also does something else that was mentioned in Chapter 4—it stops the misbehavior. Stopping the behavior is not only for that child's own good, it is also for the good of the rest of the children in class. There is an unstated attitude that we should cater only to the feelings of the misbehaving child. When a misbehaving child disrupts the class, he isn't the only person who has feelings. So do the rest of the children in that class who want to learn. (The principle of removing a misbehaving child from a situation to stop the misbehavior applies in other situations as well, such as public places and the home. Removing a disruption is good for everyone.)

Should a child have a choice whether to go in time-out? It all depends on the circumstances. If a child is upset because he is missing

---

33 Jane Nelsen, *Positive Discipline*, (New York: Ballantine Books, 1987), p. 131.
35 Jane Nelsen, *Positive Discipline*, (New York: Ballantine Books, 1987), p. 129.

his mother, and it would help him to calm down, there is no reason not to give the child a choice. However, if the child refused to stop hitting his classmates or to stop stomping on their work, he should not get a choice. He should be told he needs to take a time-out. And when he takes a time-out, it should not be a positive time-out where he gets to play with toys. He needs to sit in a spot where he can see the results of his misbehavior—the tears on the faces of the children he hurt. If the child is at home and continues to hit his brother, he should be separated from him and put in time-out where he can observe how upset he made his sibling. Or he should be sent to his room where he can be alone to mull over his behavior.

At the beginning of Chapter 1, I described a Montessori teacher who was worried that time-outs can create social problems for the offending child, so didn't put disruptive children in time-out for fear that everyone would know they were naughty. Did she really think that none of the children knew who was being naughty? Her motive was to shelter the misbehaving children by trying to hide the fact that they were misbehaving, rather than correct their inappropriate actions and protect the well-behaved children. She was more worried about social problems than moral development and safety.

It isn't time-outs that create social problems for the naughty child. It is the child's own behavior coupled with the lack of discipline. When the teacher spends all her time tending to the disruptive children, the well-behaved children resent it. And when something isn't done to stop misbehavior, the entire class is disrupted, and the children feel violated. They can't work. They are afraid. But when the offenders are removed, they feel safe. The class can carry on—they are free to learn again now that the disruption has been stopped. The focus shifts from the misbehaving children to the well-behaved children. Furthermore, the well-behaved children no longer feel threatened by the wrongdoers, so they can still be friends with them. Some people think that if a child is continuously disciplined, no one will like him, as if it were the discipline that was affecting the children's affections for each other rather than the child's own behavior. It is correction that helps children socially.

There is a fear that time-outs increase the child's separation anxiety; that they give the child the message that only his good side is acceptable, and that he is being sent away because the adult can't deal with his bad side. Adults who accept this view think the child feels shunned, so they use "time-ins" instead. As was stated in Chapter 2, time-outs are defined as a brief suspension of activity, a break, a quiet period, used especially as a disciplinary measure for children. By definition, "time-ins" are actually time-outs. The only difference is that with a "time-in," an adult sits with the child during his tantrum. Depending on the age of the child, the reason that he is upset, and the reason he was required to sit, this can be the right thing to do. In many cases, however, this is not a good idea because it rewards the child for his misbehavior by giving him more attention. In fact, the message that only his good behavior is acceptable is exactly what he needs to learn.

Appropriate discipline is not unfair; children expect parents and teachers to teach them how to behave. Positive discipline frowns on time-outs. People seem to think that time-outs come with a loud and mean tone of voice, but the standard intonation is calm and assertive. Time-outs work and they are not traumatizing, as some people think. If they are so traumatizing, why do children, without even being told they did anything wrong, come to that conclusion on their own and put themselves in time-out?[36] Time-outs give children a means to evaluate their behavior and develop self-control.

Re-direction. Positive discipline recommends using re-direction when a child needs correction. Re-direction means to change the direction of a child by distracting him or telling him to do something else. How long should re-direction go on? Jane Nelsen states, "How many times must a parent distract or redirect a child's attention? Well, as many times as it takes."[37]

Re-direction can be a valid technique. It is valid to use with toddlers who are easily distracted and who have no idea they are approaching danger or doing anything wrong. It is also valid if there is a potential problem brewing, such as several children cruising around the classroom in a loud and boisterous manner; or when a child really wants to do something and the answer is no, and the adult suggests an alternative instead.

---

36 Children who do this have been disciplined with time-outs.
37 Jane Nelson, "Distract and Direct," from her blog Positive Discipline, https://www.positivediscipline.com/distract-and-redirect

Should re-direction continue "as many times as it takes?" There are a few circumstances where this can be acceptable, such as a toddler who continues to get out of bed and must be taken back to bed over and over again. But generally, continuous re-direction, the contention that re-direction should continue until it works, is ineffective. Once children misbehave, re-direction is no longer acceptable because it distracts them away from what they have done wrong, rather than help them correct it. Continuous re-direction is too indirect. The child doesn't know he has done anything wrong, he is only told to do something else. If he continues to misbehave, nothing happens except more words from the adult. So the child learns to pay no attention to what the adult says. It disconnects him from reality.

Use of the word "no." There is a current trend to avoid using the word 'no' with children. In *How to Talk So Kids Will Listen and Listen So Kids Will Talk,* Adele Faber and Elaine Mazlish give some reasons for avoiding the use of the word "no":

> There will be many times as parents when we'll have to thwart our children's desires. Yet some children experience a blunt "No" as a call to arms, a direct attack upon their autonomy. They mobilize all their energy to counterattack. They scream, have tantrums, call names, get sullen. They barrage the parent with, "Why not?" . . . You're mean . . . I hate you!" It's exhausting even for the most patient of parents. [38]

Then they give the example of a two-year-old who wants to climb into a cradle. The mother explains that he is too big for it, but he begins to climb in anyway. She repeats that he is too big and adds that he could break it. He continues to argue, and then she says, "No!!" [39] This was considered a bad move for her to say "no." It was not.

This passage gives the impression that parents should never or rarely use the actual word "no." It is true that it is beneficial to find

38 Adele Faber and Elaine Mazlish, *How to Talk So Kids Will Listen and Listen So Kids Will Talk,*(New York: Avon Books, 1982), p. 160.

39 Adele Faber and Elaine Mazlish, *How to Talk So Kids Will Listen and Listen So Kids Will Talk,*(New York: Avon Books, 1982), p. 126.

other ways to say "no," but not because some children feel attacked, nor in order to avoid the confrontation. The reason is to get in the habit of letting the child know the reasons for the rules. When the child puts his shoes on a chair, rather than only using the word "no," it gives him more information to say, "Shoes belong on the floor. We don't want to get dirt on the furniture." But there is nothing wrong with adding the word "no" to the explanation. In the example, the mother had already given her son the reasons, given him the limits, and he chose to disobey her. For safety reasons and also to stop the arguing, she was absolutely correct to use the word "no."

David Walsh explains the importance of saying "no" to the child:

> In today's permissive society, many parents think they can't say no. They feel sometimes that they've lost their bearings on when no is appropriate and when it is heavy-handed or overprotective. Saying no is sometimes misconstrued as naysaying, of being someone with a negative attitude who simply opposes suggestions or denies permission in a reflexive mean way. But that's not what I'm talking about when I suggest you say no to your children. I'm urging you to take a strong parental stance with your children because they depend on you to help them learn to manage their desires so that someday they can do it effectively for themselves. [40]

Is the child expected to be happy at all times? Is he supposed to think he can do whatever he wants to do? Not using the word "no" does the child a great disservice. He doesn't learn how to stop, so he doesn't learn self-restraint. He doesn't learn how to deal with frustration and discontent. The ultimate consequence of this type of upbringing is the phenomena we are now seeing on college campuses— young adults who haven't learned how to handle disappointments and disagreements, and therefore can't deal with real-life situations.

Classroom meetings. Positive discipline advocates the use of class meetings (and family meetings in the home). Their purpose is for

---

40 David Walsh, *No: Why Kids—of All Ages—Need to Hear It and Ways Parents Can Say It*, (New York: Free Press, 2007), p. 5.

the children to give compliments to each other, help one another, solve problems, and plan events. [41] During these meetings, rules are decided by democratic vote, because a premise of positive discipline is that:

> [C]hildren are much more willing to follow limits they have helped create, based on their understanding of why they are necessary, and how to be responsible for them. They become effective decision-makers with healthy self-concepts when they learn to be contributing members of a family, a classroom, and society. [42]

Nelsen has suggestions for how a class meeting should be conducted. In preparation, the children are allowed to put problems, including behavior problems of individual children, on an agenda. The meetings begin with the children giving each other compliments, then during the meeting the problems on the agenda are discussed, and all the children have input. If misbehaving children are on the agenda, they are not condemned; the children learn how to state the problems and suggest solutions and "the students involved should be allowed to choose the suggestion they think would be most helpful to them." [43] It is not necessary for the teacher to enforce the decisions that the group made because if a student forgets those decisions, he will either be reminded, or the problem will go back on the agenda. [44]

Should rules be decided by a democratic vote? No. Group agreement is not proof that something is true or valid with respect to anything, including behavior. The majority can be wrong or ignorant or even tyrannical. Limits need to be set so that individuals are respected, safety is maintained, and learning continues without interruption. Rules need to be objectively determined by the adult according to the facts of reality. Can children suggest new rules or request that a rule be removed or changed? Can the adult have a meeting with the children to discuss problems? Of course, but it is

---

41 Jane Nelsen, *Positive Discipline*, (New York: Ballantine Books, 1987), p. 177.
42 Jane Nelsen, *Positive Discipline*, (New York: Ballantine Books, 1987), p. 15.
43 Jane Nelsen, *Positive Discipline*, (New York: Ballantine Books, 1987), p. 175.
44 Jane Nelsen, *Positive Discipline*, (New York: Ballantine Books, 1987), p. 200.

still the adult who makes the final decision regarding the rules, and it is the adult who enforces those rules.

Is it true that children are more willing to follow rules that they helped establish? It depends on the maturity of the children. There are some children who discuss and suggest rules, vote on them, and even sign contracts and then shortly thereafter blithely break them. The manipulative child doesn't care about following rules. His objective is to fool the adults so that he can do what he wants. The immature child can't always remember or apply rules to all contexts. Therefore, until children reach an understanding of why limits are necessary, they should not help create rules because it is nonproductive.

Should a child be allowed to choose a suggestion to improve his behavior? Again, it depends on the maturity of the child. The child who understands he has done something wrong and wants to improve will react to this approach differently than a manipulative child.

Should the behavior of unruly children be discussed by everyone at a classroom meeting? Meetings can be valuable to discuss problems when most of the class is affected or to discuss rules in a general way with the children. However, behavior problems of individual children should not be on the discussion table. Misbehaving children need to hear what they are doing that bothers other people, and to hear it from the people they are bothering, but it needs to be handled on an individual basis. Handling it where everybody gets a say is not appropriate. Proper behavior is determined objectively, not at the whims of one's peer group and not with children who may not even be involved in the problem. Children should not be learning how to control others, nor should they be learning that power over others is desirable. In addition, giving all the children the option to participate in that manner encourages them to be busybodies. Some things are none of other children's business. Some matters are a normal part of child development (such as running down a hallway instead of walking), so why draw so much attention to them? Scheduling classroom meetings every time children have squabbles with one another is a waste of time.

As far as putting a problem back on the agenda, I thought children were more likely to follow the rules that they help create. When this is not the case, the adult just needs to enforce the rules. In the classroom, the teacher needs to get on with giving lessons. Academic time should not be sacrificed to meeting after meeting. School needs to function so that learning can take place without constant interruptions. In addition, constant reminders of the rules do not help the child to remember them on his own. Instead, the child becomes dependent on someone else to do his thinking for him.

Classroom meetings correspond with John Dewey's view of discipline, "I believe that the discipline of the school should proceed from the life of the school as a whole and not directly from the teacher." [45] Allowing children to replace the teacher by voting on the rules and correcting each other's behavior is a form of peer pressure. Through the use of peer pressure (even the overuse of compliments) during these classroom meetings, children can become reliant upon what others are saying about them, rather than evaluating themselves. That is not independence.

Logical consequences. Positive discipline approves of natural consequences, but advocates avoiding the use of logical consequences because they are viewed as punishments by children and/or adults.[46] Nelsen wrote, "I now advocate not using logical consequences—at least hardly ever." [47] She explains her reasons for avoiding techniques that are viewed as punishments:

> Think of the last time you felt humiliated or treated unfairly. Did you feel like cooperating or doing better?[48]
>
> ....
>
> An example of how adults misunderstand the basic concepts of Positive Discipline is the common practice of adding humiliation to a logical consequence on the mistaken belief that children won't learn unless they *suffer* for their mistakes. [49]

---

45 John Dewey, "My Pedagogic Creed," School Journal vol. 54 (January 1897), pp. 77–80.

46 Jane Nelsen, *Positive Discipline*, (New York: Ballantine Books, 1987), p. 98. Rudolf Dreikurs, *Children: the Challenge*, (New York: Plume, 1987), p. 80. Alphie Kohn, *Punished by Rewards*, (New York: Houghton Mifflin Co., 1993), pp. 160–176.

47 Jane Nelsen, *Positive Discipline*, (New York: Ballantine Books, 1987), p. 99.

48 Jane Nelsen, *Positive Discipline*, (New York: Ballantine Books, 1987), p. 13.

49 Jane Nelsen, *Positive Discipline*, (New York: Ballantine Books, 1987), p. 27.

It is true that when humiliated or treated unfairly, one does not feel like cooperating. However, who says the child was treated unfairly? Humiliation is degrading someone else with the purpose of bringing him down and shaming him; it can be an attempt to suppress and destroy him. The purpose of discipline is not to bring a child down, but to teach the child the difference between right and wrong. It is not a humiliation, nor is it unfair, to tell a child to stop doing something harmful and then give a consequence when he doesn't stop. A correction is not the same thing as humiliation, and a child had better learn that or he will be in serious trouble later on when his employer or spouse tries to suggest that he has made a mistake. Children need to learn how to handle corrections and disagreements.

Natural consequences provide great opportunities to learn. If I don't put gas in my car, it will quit running. If I don't bring water on my hike, I could get thirsty. But learning only from natural consequences is not always sufficient. The natural consequence of not brushing one's teeth is to get cavities. Unfortunately, for the young child, he won't make the connection because the cavities come too long after the teeth weren't brushed. The natural consequence of a child running into the street without looking could be catastrophic. Some natural consequences can have long-term negative effects and others can be deadly. It should be obvious that we want to avoid those outcomes, so logical consequences are necessary.

Logical consequences are provided in other circumstances as well—to those who violate an individual's trust or right to his life. A natural consequence for a cheater is the inner knowledge that he didn't actually win; the logical, external consequence is that once people learn that he cheats, they won't invite him back for another game. A natural consequence of murder is that someone dies; an external, logical consequence is that the murderer loses the right to his own life and goes to jail. The child needs to learn that what he does can have an impact on others, and if it impacts others in a damaging way, negative consequences will be imposed on him as a result. Sheltering a child from this fact is doing nothing to prepare him for real life in the adult world.

If the consequence is clearly tied to the misbehavior, it gives the child the opportunity to learn and remember what happens when wrong actions are taken. For example, John broke a special toy that he stole from his best friend. His parents decide he should work to earn the money to replace it. They also take John over to his friend's house so that John can see for himself how sad his friend feels that his favorite toy is now unusable. John sees what happens when he does the wrong thing and learns that what he does can affect others. He also learns how to fix his mistakes. Results happen from what we do. It is a fact of life, and there is nothing wrong with parents providing logical consequences to teach children this lesson. This war against consequences is an assault against reality, the reality that the child is trying to learn.

Negotiation and/or collaboration. The positive discipline theory advocates using a process where the adult and child make decisions together about rules and what should be done when the rules are broken.

Alphie Kohn, another major proponent of positive discipline, explains the purpose of negotiation: "The more a child feels a part of the process, the more his point of view is solicited and taken seriously, the fewer problems there will be to deal with." [50] Kohn goes on to say that, unless the child is too young to participate in collaboration or unless the adult has determined that a rule is nonnegotiable, the parent should not make decisions about what the child can be expected to do. The parent must make those decisions together with the child. "Is it really wrong for children to keep their rooms messy? Must they stop grabbing toys that belong to friends? Do students in the classroom really have to raise their hands before speaking?" [51]

He is implying that rules are not objective so they need to be determined by shared opinions. This view has its roots in Dewey, for whom truth reduces to collective opinion that "emerges" from the group. Kohn is also implying that when rules are made by adults rather than through collaboration with children, they are wrong or inappropriate. There are reasons why adults make rules and, providing those rules are rational, the rules are more likely to be

---

50 Alphie Kohn, *Punished by Rewards*, (New York: Houghton Mifflin Co., 1993), p. 238.
51 Alphie Kohn, *Punished by Rewards*, (New York: Houghton Mifflin Co., 1993), p. 236.

right. Adults have had more life experience; they already know the consequences. They are responsible for helping the child learn the difference between right and wrong.

Is a child more likely to cooperate if he is allowed to negotiate a solution for misbehavior, or if he is allowed to negotiate to change the rules? That depends. It depends on the child, his age and the circumstances, and how much he understands. A child has to have adequate reasoning skills in order to negotiate. The child must be able to understand the problem and be able to think through solutions. He needs to be able to project into the future and understand cause and effect in order for anything to be resolved by talking and negotiating. If the children do negotiate and agree to a solution and then don't abide by it, the resolution should not be another talk, and another, and another. The solution is consequences instituted by the adult.

Negotiating is only appropriate to do with children who are mature enough to understand why a rule is necessary, and with things that are negotiable, and when both alternatives are acceptable to the adult. Consider this scenario: A child is jumping on the couch. In front of the couch is a coffee table and next to the couch are end tables with breakable lamps. As the child is jumping, he falls off, narrowly missing hitting his head on the coffee table, then gets back on the couch and jumps again. The parent tells him it is dangerous and tells him to stop. The child stomps his foot, "I won't." The parent says, "Well, what would you like?" The child says, "Extra snack," which is against house rules, but the parent agrees anyway. With this approach the child learns how to manipulate people in order to get what he wants. Jumping on the couch is not okay nor is an extra snack. Children cannot be allowed to negotiate over danger or morality. This kind of negotiating is permissiveness dressed up. It gives the child the impression he has a choice when he should not. The message is he can keep on doing it until the adult gives him something.

A parent may want to negotiate with a child over when he cleans his room, before or after lunch, but it is not negotiable whether or not he cleans his room. An older child, around age thirteen, refuses to clean his room, so the parent negotiates with him. The child knows that the parent doesn't like to cook, so the child suggests he fix dinner two nights a week in exchange for the parent cleaning his room. [52] That kind of trade is inappropriate. The child needs to clean his own room. It is his mess; it is his responsibility. It doesn't matter that he doesn't want to do it. We all have things in life that we don't want to do, but we do them anyway. Children need to learn that too.

The argument could be made that if adults don't want to clean, they could hire a cleaning service and that the adolescent was essentially doing the same thing by negotiating an exchange, but this isn't a situation where two adults are making a trade. One is the parent who is trying to teach a child, who is not a grown up, responsibility for his actions, and the child is trying to get out of that responsibility. In the grown-up world, hiring someone to clean does not relieve the adult from the responsibility of a clean house. The adult is still responsible to see that the job gets done.

Over-protection. Positive discipline tries to protect the child from feeling sad when disciplined. Nelsen writes: "Where did we ever get the crazy idea that in order to make children do better, first we have to make them feel worse?" [53]

Of course the goal is not to torture the child. The goal is for his happiness in the long run, but a natural consequence of doing the wrong thing, especially if it is a moral issue, is to feel remorseful. The child needs to realize that he has defied reality, to learn how to deal with his mistake, and to handle the resulting emotions.

The deep-seated fear about a child feeling unhappy when disciplined is that his self-esteem will be squelched, so adults shy away from any disciplinary action that might make the child feel sad. It is true that damage can be done to a child if the parent treats the child in a cruel, unloving manner. If the parent is continuously angry towards the child, screaming at him, and telling him explicitly that he will never amount to anything, the child may conclude the parent is correct and feel like he is worthless. That approach, however, is ridicule; it is not discipline. Proper discipline is not unloving. It is delivered in a matter of fact or kind, but firm, manner.

The fear of harming the child's self-confidence when he is corrected is based on two underlying premises: One is that self-esteem

---

52 This example was taken from: Thomas Gordon, *Parent Effectiveness Training*, (New York: Pater H. Wyden, Inc., 1970), p. 198.
53 Jane Nelsen, *Positive Discipline*, (New York: Ballantine Books, 1987), p. 13.

comes from others, and therefore one should always present a positive view to a child about himself so that he can have high self-esteem; the second is that temporary sadness or negative emotions hurt self-esteem and can cause a child to behave poorly. Both premises are false.

First, as Montessori recognized, self-esteem does not come from others. [54] The child has to earn it on his own, which takes time. The idea that saying "no" will hurt a child's self-esteem presupposes that a child already has self-esteem. A child who continues to misbehave by hitting, shoving, pushing, kicking, name-calling, and disrespecting others and property, will not feel good about himself. He does not have self-esteem; he needs to develop it.

To have a good self-image, the misbehaving child needs to change his behavior. If people are concerned about a child's self-esteem, they should learn what it is and how it is attained. Self-esteem is the result of a positive appraisal of one's self, based on one's ability to understand and deal with the real world. We need to give the child a firm and loving guiding hand so that he can develop that ability. Nothing brings self-esteem to the soul of a child more than his own competent mind.

Secondly, correction that makes a child sad will not hurt his self-esteem; feeling sad can be a constructive emotion. Emotions are a result of value judgements that a person has made; and if a child judges that he has behaved poorly, he *should* feel bad about it. How else can a child learn the difference between right and wrong unless he feels uncomfortable when he does something wrong? He can't let his "conscience be his guide" because he has been denied the development of a conscience. And if he doesn't develop a conscience, there is no self-esteem to be had.

Trying to insulate a child from all negative emotions is very harmful in the long run. Negative emotions are automatic signals that something is wrong. When things do not work out, it is necessary for the child to feel those negative emotions so that he can think about, clearly identify, and resolve the problem. If, instead, he

---

54 "[P]erfection and confidence must develop in the child from inner sources with which the teacher has nothing to do." Maria Montessori, *The Absorbent Mind*, (New York: Henry Holt and Co., 1995), p. 274.

is shielded from those feelings, he will learn that happiness is guaranteed by someone else, and, therefore, he does not have to learn or make choices and deal with the real world.

CHAPTER 6
Techniques for Proper Discipline

Discipline procedures do not require that the adult be over-bearing or controlling, nor does the adult need to intervene in each and every circumstance. Proper discipline means that the adult instructs and guides the child, helps him understand the difference between right and wrong, and decides what measures should be taken, if any, when the child misbehaves or needs help with self-control. The adult should be firm but not unkind, factual but not condescending. In this chapter I explain discipline techniques that I have found to be successful.

Set limits. The first step in the disciplinary process is to set the limits. The rules should include issues concerning safety, property, and people. Rules on other issues will vary from household to household and from classroom to classroom, depending on the individual circumstances of the people involved. Some rules will need to be adjusted as the child matures.

Give the reasons for the rules. When a child is told the rules, he must also be told the reasons for the rules. He needs to understand that reasons (not authority figures) determine rules. The child may not yet understand all the reasons, but that is okay. Giving the child a short explanation, even if the child doesn't understand, encourages his mind to be looking for reasons in the future. This process is setting the foundation for a thinking pattern later on: "Do X, because of reason Y." The long-range goal is for the child to understand the connection of rules to their rationale so that he can learn how to think rationally.

Allow time to practice. If necessary or applicable, allow time for the child to practice following the rules. If one of the rules is to refrain from throwing objects, demonstrate how to set them down gently, and then allow him to practice by repeating what you showed him. For crucial rules such as those regarding safety, or for rules that are broken repeatedly, the child needs to be told what the consequence will be if the rule is broken again.

Evaluate the context when a child misbehaves. When a child behaves inappropriately, the adult must first evaluate the context. Then the options can be considered and it can be determined if actions should be taken. (Evaluating the context can be challenging for some adults at first, but it gets better with practice.)

Here are some questions to ask yourself: What are the circumstances? Was this the first time he broke this particular rule or does he repeatedly break it? Did he do it on purpose? If it was an accident, was he being careless? Does he need another presentation of the lesson? Does he need some discipline in order to help him get some body control? Is he upset about something that can be corrected without discipline (e.g. his socks are too small for his feet and he is whining because of it)?

Learn how to read a child. Is the child tired? Is he hungry? Is he sick? Is his sense of order upset? Is he having trouble communicating what he wants to say? Is someone doing something for the child that he is already able to do for himself and he is frustrated? Does the child want something that he can't have? Does the child wish to change reality? Is he testing reality? Is he testing an adult? Is he manipulating an adult or are his tears genuine? Is he a sensitive child? How does he relate to the other children? Is he trying to control someone? And so on.

Treat each child as an individual. Unlike the view of Dreikurs, each child needs to be judged and treated as an individual. With some children in class, all it takes is "the look" to get them back on task. Some distractible children may need only a reminder while others may need a special place to work away from distractions. Children who regularly test the limits may need to go to time-out. Or, if they can't concentrate while working with a friend, they may need to be told to wait a week before working with that friend again. Sensitive children may need encouragement along with a hug. Some children respond well to humor, and if they are having a grumpy streak of uncooperativeness, a little playfulness can lighten their mood and change their attitude.

Use consequences to help with self-control. In determining if a consequence should be given, be realistic about what children are capable of doing. One can't take an infant to a concert and expect the child to be quiet. But consequences can help an older child to develop body awareness and gain self-control. Some classrooms start and/or end the day with all the children sitting on a line. When new children start school, it is not uncommon for some of them to be unable to sit still while sitting on the line, especially the two- and three-year-olds. Wiggling around while sitting is a distraction to the other children, but those wigglers should not be sent to time-out (unless they irritate the children sitting next to them by touching or hitting), because they lack the ability to sit still. But when dismissing them from the line, the teacher should not call their names until they are sitting still, with legs folded and hands in their lap. At first, it will only be for a few seconds that they can sit still before being called, but it is a start, and eventually, after a few months, they will be very proud that they are able to sit like the others. An eight-year-old confirmed that this works, saying to her former teacher, "You know how I learned to sit still when I was in your class? Because you didn't call on me until I was sitting like the other children."

Use choice-making. Once you have determined the context and that the child needs correction, before taking any disciplinary action, it is usually beneficial to first give the child a chance to change his behavior by giving him a choice. "Your choice is to either stop screaming or go to your room." If the child rejects that choice or insists on one that is unacceptable, he needs to be told that if he doesn't choose one of the options he was given, the adult will choose one for him. The child may continue to scream without going to his room, in which case the adult has to follow through and escort the child to his room. If the child refuses to stay in his room, the parent needs to hold the door shut.

Don't give a choice to a child when you don't mean it. Don't say, "Would you like to finish picking up your toys?" It is better to say, "It's time to pick up your toys." But if you want to give the child a choice, you could say: "Would you like to pick up your toys before or after you eat your snack?" But if he chooses to do it after his snack, make sure that he does it, or giving choices won't mean anything to him.

Choice-making gives the child a chance to stop and think about what he is doing. If he changes his behavior, he learns that he can control his actions. Children need experience in making choices so that they can differentiate between right and wrong. Offering choices to a child is important in teaching him to consider alternatives, which he needs to learn how to do in order to have good behavior. This does not mean giving a child unlimited choices; choices must be limited to those that are safe, age-appropriate, and commonsensical. A child cannot be given choices regarding things he knows nothing about. Asking him to make an unqualified decision makes him feel insecure. If a child is misbehaving at school, and he expresses that he dislikes his school, he should not be asked what school he would like to attend instead. He does not have enough knowledge to know what he needs to know when he grows up and which school will give him that knowledge. Plus, if the school is justified in its concerns about his behavior, giving him the choice to change schools will not persuade him to face up to what he has done nor encourage him to learn better behavior. On the other hand, if the school is not justified in its concerns about the child and is dealing with him unfairly, a change may be good, but the parents still need to make that choice, not the child.

Counting. If a child refuses to clean up his mess or put on his coat (assuming that the child is capable of doing it independently), the adult can count to ten. Counting is effective because even though it is difficult for the child to understand time, he quickly learns how long it takes to get to ten. Then sometimes all the adult has to do is start counting and the child begins to move. However, if the action isn't done by the time the parent gets to ten, there needs to be a consequence, and it may be a natural consequence, rather than a logical one. When Lori was three years of age, she would not put her coat on before going to school. Her mother explained it was cold outside and that they would be leaving as soon as she was done counting. Mother told her if she didn't get it on, she would have to go without her coat, but Lori continued to procrastinate. So when Mother was done counting to ten, she put on her own coat and put Lori in her car seat without hers. It was winter time and it was cold outside, but not so cold that it would be harmful, so Mother didn't turn on the heat in the car. Soon she heard a little voice in the back seat, "M... m-m-mommy, I'm c...c-cold!" Mother said, "I am so sorry that you decided not to put on your coat." Mother never had a problem with Lori putting on her coat again.

Time-outs. If you decide to put the child in a time-out, he needs to sit long enough for him to calm down so that he can think about what he did and why it was wrong. Many adults use the "one minute for every year of a child's age" rule (the child sits one minute for every year of his life). This usually isn't enough. [1] If you put a four-year-old in a chair for four minutes, he often gets up and immediately misbehaves again. When a child sits in time-out, the adult should not let him get up until he sits still without crying, screaming, or goofing around. However, some children, if mature enough, can be allowed to release themselves from the chair once they are sitting calmly and quietly.

If a student refuses to go to the time-out chair, the teacher needs to move him to a chair. If the child keeps getting out of the chair and runs around, the teacher needs to hold him in the chair. After once or twice, most children will get the message that the adult means it, and will stay there on their own.

Here is an example. Thomas, age 4, kept getting out of his chair and disrupting students who were working. The assistant tried to convince him to stay in the chair. "The children don't like it when you bother them." Then the boy started to hit the assistant. Again, she tried to reason with him. "You are setting the wrong example." "That isn't nice." "That hurts."

The teacher walked over to him and brought him over by her, sat him in a chair and held him there. "Let me go!" he yelled, as he attempted to kick, hit, and bite her.

"No," she said. "Not until you calm down. You have to sit in this chair until you can show us that you are ready to go to work."

---

1 For an 18-month-old, one minute is enough.

This went on for about fifteen minutes. At last Thomas started to relax, she let go of him, and he sat quietly and calmly. They talked about why he was in the chair, and then the teacher told him he could go back to work as long as he obeyed the rules. He was good for the rest of the day until the end of class when he started running around. She told him to go to the chair and he did. And he stayed there.

Avoid lectures. At the time a child is disciplined, some adults will give the child a long lecture about his wrongdoing: why it was wrong, what will happen if he keeps doing it, what he should do instead, and so on. These long dissertations need to be avoided. This is also not the time to try to "reason" with him. That comes later. During these long verbal exchanges, the child will try to grasp the meaning of the words (because of his sensitivity to language, birth to age 5) rather than try to understand his behavior. Give the child your reasons ("You could fall and hurt yourself."), but don't expect immediate results. In time he will see you are right, and your reasons for what you say prepare him for logic. But logic doesn't work yet. (If I continue to run in the room with the blocks, I could trip and fall, that would hurt, etc.) When an adult lectures and lectures, some children misbehave again because of the attention they receive. Other children, however, react differently. Since the only consequence for their misbehavior is the flow of words, they tune out the monologues.

Keeping quiet at the appropriate times is valuable. At our Montessori school, the children are allowed to eat a snack at a specific table with room for four children to sit. Children must remain seated while eating, otherwise other children might take their place, which creates conflict among the children. A child gets up from the snack table and runs around. The teacher reminds him of the rule, but he continues to get up and run. So she says, "Next time you get out of your chair, you're done." The child gets up again and the adult removes the snack *without a word*. Removing the food in silence teaches the child to listen.

Talk to the child afterwards. When a child is given a consequence for misbehavior, in most cases, the adult needs to talk to the child afterwards to make sure that he understands why he was disciplined. Ask him what happened and how he felt about it. Ask him to tell you what he did that was wrong and to explain why it was wrong. If he doesn't remember what he did or why it was wrong, explain it to him. You can also ask him why he disobeyed the rule. Usually the child doesn't know why, but it is still okay to ask because it will encourage him to think about it. And if he is able to give you a reason, such as, "I was mad at John," you can also talk about that with him. Last, discuss a better way to handle the situation. If the child is young and is just beginning to learn social skills, tell him what to do: "If John calls you a baby again, tell him he hurt your feelings, that you are not a baby, and that calling you a baby was not okay. If that doesn't work, come and get me and I will handle it." If the child is older and has some knowledge about what he should do, ask: "If John calls you a baby again, what do you think you could do instead?"

Sometimes children will refuse to talk to the adult. If the child puts his hands over his ears, this is rude and should not be tolerated. Shutting people out is not an acceptable way to treat reasonable, caring people who want to communicate with you. If a child is being belligerent and defiant, the adult needs to insist that he answer. Perhaps tell him he can't go outside and play until he talks to you. If the child is frightened and timid say, "I need to talk to you about this because I want to help you, but I can't if you won't tell me what's wrong (or what John did). If you decide to talk to me, come find me and I will listen." Sometimes the emotional, sensitive child just needs some more time to calm down and think about what happened.

Length of logical consequences. If you decide to give a child a logical consequence, the length of time of the consequence will depend on the child and the circumstances. You may have to keep trying until you find what works.

Cassie's parents had to keep increasing the length of a consequence in order to get her to stop an unsafe act. When Cassie was four or five years of age she used to love to get the mail from the mail box in front of her house. As she made her way to the mailbox, she would also run out into the street without looking for cars. The parents tried banning her from getting the mail for short periods of time, but it didn't work so they banned her for one year. It worked. After the end of that year, she never ran out into the street again.

People voiced concern that the long-term consequence would make Cassie sad and damage her self-esteem. When she was seven years of age, her mother asked her if she remembered why they wouldn't let her get the mail. "Because I kept running out in the street and you were worried I might get hit by a car." When asked how long she had been banned, she replied, "It was a *long* time! A week!"

Note that she remembered the reason, but not the time. Her parents wanted to make a big impression on her and succeeded. Note also the fallacy of "making them sad will destroy their self-esteem." Yes, she was unhappy when she couldn't go get the mail, but discipline is not about keeping them happy all the time. In the long run they will be happy if they develop self-control. Also note that a dead child is neither happy nor does that child have self-esteem. When it comes to an issue of morality or safety, adults must be unwavering in their approach with the child—do not be afraid to do what it takes.

Public corrections. Some teachers who use positive discipline are opposed to public corrections in the classroom. Whether or not a child should be disciplined in front of other people depends on what the child did, where it happened, and how the discipline is done. If the incident involves only the child, it should be handled with only that child; if it involves two children, it should be handled with just those two children. In a family, however, almost everyone knows what everyone else is doing and how they are behaving. Due to the closeness of the relationships, corrections can't all be done privately. In a classroom, while not as intimate as a family, the same principle applies.

If a student breaks a rule and creates a major disruption, the teacher needs to handle it right there on the spot. If the child feels embarrassed or remorseful about what he did, or if he needs help with something he is upset about, depending on that child's personality, the teacher may need to talk with him privately. If one child is furious with a friend and the friend is crying, it might be a good idea to talk to them privately. But so much depends on the circumstances.

Trying to embarrass a child in a public setting, in order to get him to change, is a bad idea. Not only is it unkind, it encourages him to focus on what others think of him. It makes no sense, for example, for a parent to speak to a child about the fact that his room is a dirty mess in front of his friends during a birthday party. Does the parent think the child will leave the party and rush right home and clean it? Making negative remarks about the child's appearance is insensitive and not helpful, "What's wrong with you? You're as skinny as a rail. You eat like a bird." Or, "Get that hair out of your eyes. You look horrible." If a child is having trouble learning a skill, statements like this from the teacher will not motivate him to work harder: "You never practice your handwriting. I can't even read your sloppy letters. When are you ever going to learn how to use that pencil correctly? Can't you ever do anything that I ask you to do?" Speaking to a child in this manner is demeaning and inappropriate. Attempting to shame a child does nothing to persuade him to improve. Instead it discourages him.

When Charlene was in seventh grade, a popular trick to play on a friend was to push her head down while she was taking a drink at the water fountain. The students all thought it was a hilarious prank. One day after gym class, Charlene pulled the prank on her friend, Jane, but this time the response was not laughter. Instead of raising her head with a wet face, Jane raised her head with a chipped tooth! Charlene was devastated. The next day in art class the art teacher went on a tirade about this horrible kid who had chipped her friend's tooth, and how she needed to be punished severely. Since the teacher did not mention that it was an accident, the implication was that Charlene had done it on purpose. Although she didn't mention Charlene's name, everyone knew who it was and turned around in their seats to look at her. Her rant went on and on for what seemed like forever to Charlene. The regret that Charlene felt for what she had done was already unbearable enough; she didn't need any more guilt piled onto her; she had learned her lesson. This isn't to say that just because Charlene felt bad, that the principal and her parents didn't need to talk to her about it. It also didn't mean that Charlene didn't have to make amends for what she had done, like earn the money to pay the dental bill. But she didn't need the public humiliation to get her to realize that she had done the wrong thing.

Let's say the circumstances were different. What if Charlene thought a chipped tooth was funny and didn't care that she had hurt her friend? What if she even did it on purpose and then bragged about this fact to the other students? She would need to be told, in the presence of those students, that this isn't at all funny, and she had committed a serious offense. In addition, something would need to be said to the rest of the class so that they know she didn't get away with it, that justice was done.

Situations can pop up in the classroom that need to be handled in front of everyone, but teachers can worry too much about children's feelings and bend over backwards in order to protect the wrongdoer from being identified and any resulting unhappy feelings and emotional melt-downs. But avoiding melt-downs will not help children with emotional fragility learn how to handle their feelings. In addition, with this over-protection, they can miss valuable teaching moments.

At school we used to have a gift exchange at Christmas time, and occasionally a child was unhappy with the gift he received. Jake, a highly emotional child, angrily announced loudly and sharply that he didn't like the gift he received from Andrea. Andrea burst into tears. This had no effect on Jake who continued to rant on and on about how much he hated the gift.

Children are learning social skills for the very first time and are unaware of how something like that sounds to the gift giver. Just like when they are out in public and announce that someone is fat, they have no idea how that statement affects the person described. Their context of how and why a gift is given is limited. This is how I handled that situation: I turned to Jake and said, "Oh? I like it because…" If I didn't like it, I wouldn't lie; instead I found something positive to say about it. "I understand that you don't like it, but that ornament might look nice on your Christmas tree." And I would also say, "I am so sorry that you don't like the gift. Andrea didn't know that you wouldn't like it when she gave it to you." When Jake continued to make more negative remarks, I stopped him immediately. I told him that he didn't have to like the gift, but he was saying hurtful things to Andrea. If necessary, I would have him look right at Andrea so he could see her tears and point out how his remarks hurt her feelings.

I couldn't ignore it, nor could I speak to Jake in private. All the children were there, they all saw and heard what happened. I couldn't hide from the children the fact that Jake did something wrong. I couldn't pretend it didn't happen when it did happen. I couldn't prevent it from being out in the open when it was already out in the open. If I spoke to Jake privately about it, I would not be sticking up for Andrea publicly. Justice would not have been done, and justice is something children want and need. There are times when you speak to children privately about things, but this wasn't one of those times.

This approach worked. It satisfied all the children. I acknowledged that Jake didn't have to like the gift, but that it was wrong to respond to his friend with rudeness. I acknowledged Andrea's hurt feelings, so she felt heard and understood. They all learned a little that day about gift giving. They learned that friends do not try to give you something that you don't like; that when you don't like a gift, it is not okay to go overboard in expressing it and hurt your friend. And Jake didn't have a melt-down; he even gave Andrea a hug later that day. I have found that most children appreciate honesty and bluntness. Honesty and bluntness can be delivered gently and firmly, without being mean or angry.

Whether corrections are done publicly or privately depend on the children and the circumstances, and the circumstances can be complicated, but that is what makes working with children so challenging…and fun.

Do not force children to apologize. It is a very common practice for adults to insist that children apologize when they have done something wrong. Adults often teach the child to apologize by hovering nearby, prompting the child by saying, "What do you have to say to Jimmy?" or, worse yet, "Tell him you're sorry." Some adults even follow the child and watch to make sure that the apology is properly delivered. The goal of forced apologies is to convince the child of his wrong doing, for the child to feel remorse and to make amends. Learning when and how to apologize when one is genuinely sorry is a necessary and valid social skill. However, forcing children to apologize is a form of humiliation and is, therefore, a form of punishment. In addition, forced apologies are unproductive and likely to be harmful.

Frequently, adults insist the apology be delivered immediately following a misbehavior. For example, the teacher sees Katy hit Jimmy, and wants to step in and insist that Katy apologize. At that moment,

Katy is still very angry, which is why she hit in the first place. Forcing her to say she is sorry will teach her two things. One, it will teach her to repress her anger, because it gives the message that anger is not okay. Two, it will teach her to lie since, at that moment, she is *not* sorry for what she did. So what should be done in this situation?

It is important to identify, or help Katy to identify, exactly what her feelings are. This can be done by asking questions such as, "Did Jimmy call you a name? Is that why you hit him?" Her feelings can be validated by confirming that anger is a normal and acceptable reaction to name-calling. Then she needs to understand that there may be better ways to resolve the difficulty—"Can you think of any, Katy?"—and help her to find some, such as saying to Jimmy, "That hurt my feelings, Jimmy. Don't call me stupid."

When the child has calmed down and can see that the anger is understood and accepted, then making amends can be suggested with words such as, "Is there anything you'd like to say to Jimmy?" This gives Katy an opening through which she can apologize. She may or may not respond in a positive way, but the opportunity has been provided for her to talk. That's all some children need to be able to honestly say, "I'm sorry."

Another common pattern that occurs when children are forced to apologize is misbehavior immediately followed by the child's insisting, "I'm sorry! I'm sorry!", thereby, in his mind, making everything okay. In such a short interval, however, he can neither have admitted his anger nor experienced remorse. What he is hoping is that his "apology" will keep him out of trouble. When the adult expresses displeasure he pleads, "But I said I was sorry!!!"

Like Katy and Jimmy in the example above, this child needs help in understanding that anger is okay, but expressing it inappropriately and then offering a meaningless apology is not okay. In fact, the apology constitutes a lie. The child needs first to feel the remorse and understand the need to change his behavior. Only then will "I'm sorry" be valid.

At times it is apparent that the child is genuinely sorry for what he has just done. In this case too, validation is important. "I can see that you feel bad about what you did." Then explain, "When we've done something wrong we can go to the person we hurt and say we're sorry. Sorry means you feel bad about what you did and that you're going to try and make things better." Then leave it up to the child to decide what to do. Being forced to speak at that moment could provide an extremely humiliating experience for him. If it appears that he does want to apologize at once, he may need the adult to come along for moral support; but it is more likely that he will wait until the adults are absent. Apologizing is a personal, private matter, an uninvited audience is inappropriate. The wise adult will allow the child to learn that through experience.

Humiliating a child by forcing him to apologize does not convince him of his wrong doing. Instead, it teaches the child to repress his anger and to lie, and the child learns it is ok to misbehave as long as he says he is sorry. Forced apologies should not be done.

Defiant children in the classroom. One big mistake teachers make is the belief that if they can just get the disobedient children to behave, the rest of the class will flow smoothly—as if their class isn't functioning well because of those particular children. So teachers bend over backwards in hopes that things will improve. They sit with individual disruptive children outside the classroom every day hoping to calm them down, pleading with them to behave, or use other measures which take the teacher away from the rest of the class. Why is there all this attention and sympathy given to the disruptive children? What about the rest of the students? Of course, teachers worry about those defiant children and want them to be successful, but giving children lots of extra attention for misbehavior doesn't work.

Teachers must not allow the disruptive children to ruin their class; insolent children should not be their main focus. It isn't fair to them, to the teacher and, most of all, to the other children. The main focus should be taking measures so that learning is not disrupted for the class as a whole. It is utterly unfair to give defiant children priority over the rest of the children who want to learn.

Make it clear to the disruptive, insolent child through your attitude and actions that it is not your problem if he continues to misbehave; it is his problem. Provide the discipline and guidance for him to change, and change becomes his responsibility. Don't worry if he sits in the chair every day. He needs to develop self-control and he needs to learn proper behavior by observing the correct behavior of the rest of the children in class. He can do that while sitting; he can't do it while he is running around the room. This approach works because the misbehaving children are not allowed to sabotage the learning of the rest of the children, and eventually the disruptive ones come around.

Sometimes all it takes is to be super firm right from the beginning. On Calvin's first day of school he was extremely defiant. The teacher told him what the rules were and the reasons for the rules, but he refused to follow them. He would break those rules on purpose while sneering at her behind her back. He would wait until she wasn't looking and throw items or step on someone's work. This was a distraction to the rest of the students who were trying to work. At the end of class, the children would put their work away and sit on a line in order to be dismissed. He refused, "But I don't want to sit on the line," he shouted. Her response: "Well, you have to." And when he ran away from her, she caught him and brought him back to the line. Then she told him she didn't care what he wanted; he should obey the rules. At the end of class he went home and told his parents that he had a great time at school and talked about his teacher the rest of the day. From that day forward, he was respectful towards his teacher and became a delightful student. This was one of those times when the teacher needed to temporarily come across as an authoritarian. Calvin was being overtly insolent as he tested her and was disrupting the class as he did so. But once he knew the parameters of what was permissible, he felt secure and began to cooperate, and the teacher resumed her usual authoritative stature.

Then there are the children who are frightened and angry and refuse to cooperate. Chad would sit by himself at the beginning of class time and mope. He would constantly refuse the teacher when she told him she had work to show him. So she put on her authoritarian shoes, carried him kicking and screaming over to the shelf to get work, showed him how to do it, and then insisted he do it. Then she told him he couldn't get up until he did the work, and he would sit for days in a stubborn funk. When she contacted his parents about his uncooperativeness, they told her that he was also impossible at his previous school. He would throw fits and cry, and the teachers didn't know how to handle him. So, she persevered and continued to insist that he do his work. Little by little, he began to change. Through his work he started to develop some confidence. One year later, rather than crying when the teacher told him she had new work to show him, he was asking her for new work, came up with his own ideas for work, and even told her that he wanted to learn how to read. His concentration improved dramatically, and he became a very happy boy.

What about the child who gets enjoyment by injuring others, smirks when he makes someone cry, destroys property on purpose, is disrespectful towards all adults, or does something atrocious to hurt himself? What if that child refuses to sit in time-out and the teacher ends up holding him in the chair day after day, week after week with no results? While the Montessori method greatly benefits special needs children, a child who continues to be insolent and defiant needs more help than the classroom teacher can give him; he needs additional help, and he needs to get it outside of school. Teachers are not psychologists, nor do they have the time to be. Classrooms are not therapy sessions. Time should not be taken up with continuous classroom meetings for behavior problems. The job of the teacher is to educate children. It is the parents' responsibility to start discipline before the child starts school and get the child to the point where he can function in a classroom setting. If the child does not respond to appropriate disciplinary procedures, trusted professionals need to be consulted.[2]

The child who acts like he doesn't care. Some children don't seem to care when disciplined. As an example, Mike was leaning back in his chair, so his mom told him that if he continued to do it, he would have to stand by the table while eating instead of sitting. He continued to lean his chair back, so she took it away, and he laughed, thinking it was funny. The mom was concerned, but the goal was accomplished, which was to keep him safe. It doesn't matter if he thinks it is funny. (She could tell him she doesn't think it is funny if she wanted.) After days or weeks, if he is still standing, he will get tired of it and won't think it is funny anymore and will be motivated to change.

---

2 The place to start is with the child's pediatrician to rule out any physical ailments.

Be consistent. Consistency is probably the most important aspect of discipline because if you aren't consistent, the child will stop listening to you. Always follow through and do what you said you were going to do. If you tell a child that he will need to go to time-out if he hits again, send him to time-out if he hits again. If you tell him he needs to go to his room because of a misbehavior, make sure he goes there. If for some reason you can't or are unable to follow through, explain why, but it had better be a really good reason, such as an emergency.

Be patient. Some children seem to understand why they shouldn't do something, but they do it anyway. Don't let it discourage you. Does the child truly understand? Or is he testing? Or is it because he hasn't developed enough self-control? Adolescents impulsively do some things they know are wrong, but do it anyway, pushing away the possible consequences of their actions in their minds. Self-control can be hard, even for an adult. If your doctor tells you not to eat chocolate because of a medical condition, you may very well understand all the reasons why you shouldn't eat it, but it still may be hard to resist eating truffles.

Some adults give up when their attempt at discipline doesn't work. At conference time some parents would complain, "I sent him to his room and it didn't work, so I quit doing it." All children are different, and some listen better than others; some observe closely and learn quicker, but proper behavior takes time to learn—eighteen to twenty-one years of time.

CHAPTER 7
Children and Conflict

Why do children have social conflicts? Why do they argue and/or fight? And what should adults do when children ask for help? Authoritarians think the adult should control the situation and solve the problems for the child, but this encourages dependence rather than independence; the child will not learn how to solve his own problems. Those who have been influenced by Dewey think the problems should be handled by the group, which also encourages dependence. Some people think that the adult should stay completely out of children's fights. Dreikurs explains why he thinks adults should refrain from getting involved:

> It may be hard to believe, but this is the purpose of the fighting—it drives Mother "crazy".[1]

> Whatever the reason behind the children's fights, parents only make matters worse when they interfere, try to solve the quarrel, or separate the children. Whenever a parent interferes in a fight he is depriving children of the opportunity for learning how to resolve their own conflicts. We all experience situations in which there are conflicts of interests, and all of us have to develop skills in dealing with conflict situations. We have to learn the give and take of life.[2]

---

1 Rudolf Dreikurs, *Children: the Challenge*, (New York: Plume, 1987), p. 204.
2 Rudolf Dreikurs, *Children: the Challenge*, (New York: Plume, 1987), pp. 204–205.

What if the children are engaging in physical violence?

> If our interference in the fight satisfies the children, why
> should they stop fighting? If a fight yields no result other
> than a bruise or even a bloody nose (which will mend),
> won't the child be more inclined to resolve his conflict in
> another manner? [3]

Is he right? Should adults stay out of their fights? It depends. Children do not automatically know how to resolve conflict, and it is our job as parents and teachers to teach them. Whether or not adults give assistance depends on the personalities of the children involved, what they are fighting about, and the manner in which they are fighting.

Adults should not stay out of fights that involve physical violence, damage to property, and/or emotional or psychological damage (i.e., bullying). The child will not be more inclined to resolve the fight differently if the adult stays out of it. Children need to learn that it is okay to be angry, but it is not permissible to hit, bite, punch, threaten, or harm anyone else in any manner. To allow it means it is acceptable. A child once said to a teacher: "Well, you saw us do it and didn't do anything about it so we thought it was okay to do." Children make judgements about what is permissible behavior by what adults permit.

When children fight, it isn't always to get attention from their parents. Nor do they fight because they aren't good by nature, as some people seem to think. The main reason they argue is because they take reality seriously and are trying to figure things out. They are confronting many new experiences and they want to know what is true and what isn't true. As they are figuring this out, they make errors. Then they announce their conviction and another child disagrees. For both children, their sense of order is upset. Add to that the fact that they think when someone says something, that makes it true, and the problem is magnified. So they argue. "There are four 'Home Alone' movies." "No, there aren't." Or they come running to the adult: "Miss Char! Stephanie says I don't have a dog and I do! Do I?" "John says my picture isn't pretty. Is it?"

---

3 Rudolf Dreikurs, *Children: the Challenge*, (New York: Plume, 1987), p. 205.

When children argue over the facts of reality, ask them questions to get them to think about it. "How do you know there are four movies?" "Why do you think he is saying that you don't have a dog?" "What do *you* think about your picture?" Try to get the child to come to conclusions on the facts based on his own observations. However, if a child is just trying to be silly or argumentative by denying the truth, say, "Yes, Stephanie, she has a dog." When there are other disagreements about facts, tell the child how he can find out. "Go count the addition beads and see how much two plus two is." If there is no other way for the child to figure out the answer to a factual question, such as "What color is that?" the adult needs to answer.

Children can form the wrong conclusions and some of those conclusions need to be corrected immediately. "Elyse doesn't like me." "How do you know?" the teacher asked. "Because she walked away from me while we were looking at books." The child doesn't know that there could be other reasons why she walked away. "Go ask Elyse why she walked away." When the child came back, the teacher asked, "What did she say?" "She said she went to get a drink of water." Children need to learn that they need to find more information before forming a conclusion.

"No one likes me. Josh doesn't want to work with me," said Cory, a shy, unassertive child. Children make assumptions and if the supposition is made that no one likes them, it will affect their future relationships negatively. "I think you should ask Josh why he doesn't want to work with you." And knowing Cory's fearful personality, the teacher added, "Do you need my help?" "Yes," said Cory. The teacher called Josh over to them. Cory asked him why and Josh said, "I just want to work by myself for a while." Josh was asked, "So you are still friends with Cory then? Do you still like him?" "Yes."

When children claim that no one likes them, it could be because they think that in order to be friends, the friends must be together all the time. This is a common misconception. It could also be the case that the child simply has a short memory or is confusing his feelings with reality. If a child claims that no one likes him and then sometime later he is doing a project with a friend, this needs to be pointed out to him. "I thought you said no one liked you and that no one wants to work with you. Cameron is working with you right now."

Sometimes children don't even know what the word "friend" means: Anna, a four-year-old, was upset because Alan, age five, said he wasn't her friend. So I called Alan over and he confirmed that he had said that. I asked him, "Do you know what the word 'friend' means?" "No," he replied. So I asked him if he had any friends in the class and he named three boys. Then I said, "Why are they your friends? What does friend mean?" He said, "If you just want to play, or do something, or do a booklet, or that stuff." Then I explained that you can have a friend and not see him or work with him, and he said, "Oh yeah, like Jim. I'm not with him all the time." So I said, "Do you think you could be friends with Anna?" He said that yes, she could be his friend, but he didn't want to work with her that day.

"Cory says I'm mean. Am I?" The child needs to know what, if anything, he did that was mean, so Josh needs to go back and ask him what he meant. If Cory thought that Josh was mean because he wanted to work alone, the adult needs to reassure Josh that working alone is not mean. In other cases, when the adult knows what happened or is dealing with a mature, knowledgeable child, "Did you do anything mean?" "No." "Go back and tell him you didn't do anything mean."

Occasionally a child complains that no one wants to work with him and it may be true. In those situations, the children need to be encouraged to tell him exactly why. "You get in my face." "You keep touching my work and I told you to stop." The offending child isn't going to change his behavior if he doesn't know what he is doing that bothers the other children. Children actually think about how to interact properly. A child in my class said this to another child, "Can I watch you if I be nice to you? If I not be nice, then I can't watch you?"

Then there is this grievance, "Sally won't be my friend." Some children are genuinely disturbed by this and others come demanding that the adult fix it. It can't be fixed. The adult cannot force friendships and should not try. Adults would rebel if they were forced to be friends with someone they didn't like; why is it acceptable to force relationships on children? Children have to respect the individual rights of others, but they do not have to like everyone. The purpose of school is to learn, not to have friends. Friends are a value and a very important one, but a child cannot have meaningful relationships without knowledge and self-confidence. That comes first.

If a child seems sincerely upset about Sally and her lack of friendship, offer your sympathy and understanding. "I can see you are sad. Did you ask Sally why she doesn't want to be your friend?" Or suggest solutions, "Maybe you could ask Rory if you could eat lunch with her today." "Can you think of someone else to work with today?" If a child pressures the adult to solve his problem, the adult can say, "I can't force children to be friends with each other." Or, "She doesn't have to be your friend." Or, if applicable, "You need to start being nice to her and then maybe she'll be your friend."

As they form friendships, they will try to figure out how to get their friends to do what they want them to do, so they may try to control them. "You won't be my best friend if..." or "You can't come to my birthday party unless you..." They don't understand that you can have more than one friend, so when their friend wants to be with someone else, their feelings can get hurt. Most children will learn with experience that they can't control other people, and that friends don't have to be together all the time, but if one child is being too controlling and overbearing with a timid, unassertive child, the adult needs to intervene. The unassertive child may need some coaching on how to speak up and say what he really wants. Or the overbearing child may need to be stopped when he tries to boss his friend around; children should not get in the habit of trying to control others. Both children are dependent on one another and may need to be separated for periods of time so that they see they will be fine on their own.

Property and ownership issues are common ignitors of contention. Children learn about reality by using objects, so they will fight over possessions. They often want to do what another child is doing and find it hard to refrain from interfering. The school and home environments need to be structured in such a way that respects the rights of the child. If the adult wants children to learn how to get along, there is a very important principle that needs to be followed— children should not be forced to share.

When adults approve of one child grabbing an object away from another child, in the name of sharing, they are allowing bullying behavior. It is not okay to take something from someone else without his permission. That is stealing. And it is abhorrent to expect the victim to cooperate and be friendly toward the thief. Children who are forced to share will fight, because they learn not to trust one another and come to view each other as threats, rather than as having value. Why is the child who wants the toy more important than the child who wants to keep his toy?

In the Montessori classroom there is no forced sharing. When a child takes out an activity to work on, it is his until he puts it away. No one is allowed to touch his work unless he is invited. This bothers some children at first, and requires us to enforce the rule, but they do learn and accept it. They come to understand that noninterference is showing respect for the other person and that they will get the same respect in return. Children will share on their own when they are ready, but it has to be their choice. (For some suggestions on how to handle sharing in the home, see Appendix 2.)

Children can also have conflict in their social relationships because they lack communication skills. They don't know what to say or do in order to resolve problems, and may end up hitting in frustration and anger. "Did you kick her?" "Well, I don't like her." Or they may hit because they like someone. "I was just trying to get his attention." Some children may say something in order to get a rise out of their friend in a hurtful manner when their friend doesn't do what they think he should. It helps to teach children how to use "I-messages": "I feel hurt because you won't work with me."[4] "I like you and would like to be your friend." Then allow the children to role play and practice.

In class, it can be helpful to have an artificial flower to use when the children are upset with each other.[5] The child who is upset can take the flower to his friend and tell him what was bothering him, then hand the flower to his friend to respond. Only the child who has the flower can talk. They hand the flower back and forth, talking to each other until they resolve the problem. Children can resolve their own problems once they have enough knowledge (it is against the rules to step on work because it can be destroyed) and communication skills ("I felt upset when you messed up my work.").

---

4 The idea of "I-messages" came from Thomas Gordon, *Parent Effectiveness Training*, (New York: Peter H. Wyden, Inc., 1970), pp. 103–121.
5 Montessori schools often refer to this flower as the "peace rose."

When children do not have the knowledge or the skills, children may need the adult to help them discuss the problem, figure out who or what was wrong, and come to a resolution. In this case, each child needs to tell his side of the story. The younger child (age 3) has a difficult time visualizing the sequence of events, so it is usually hard for him to explain what happened. If the teacher cannot determine what happened for sure, she can call over reliable, mature children who witnessed the event for verification.

If the teacher cannot figure out what happened, and if there were no witnesses, she can acknowledge that the children are upset and re-state the rule. "I don't know what happened. I wish I could help you. I know you are both upset about whatever happened. Lauren, I don't know whether you hit Shelly or not, but if you did, we don't hit. It is okay to be angry, but hitting hurts people. If you are angry with Shelly, tell her why instead." Stating a general fact usually ends the matter.

Children can be very upset, as if the world is coming to an end, but as each child tells his side of the story, they start to calm down, think more clearly, and are able to come to a resolution. For most children, this works, but if the story keeps changing with an older child (age 5 or 6), chances are he is lying and doesn't want to take responsibility for what he did. If so, the teacher cannot let him get away with this. She needs to confront him with the lie, point out his participation in the wrongdoing, and explain why it was wrong.

Learning how to resolve conflict is a part of the process of grow-ing up, and some childhood relationships can be very volatile—one moment two children are best friends, the next moment enemies, then best friends again the next day. The volatility can be minimized, however, once adults understand the nature of the child, and respect and enforce his rights. While it can be difficult to know when to step in and when to let the children work it out for themselves, it is very important for children to learn the process of problem solving on their own. Problems need to be dealt with through truth and reason, rather than by group consensus as advocated by John Dewey. Don't be too quick to interfere; sometimes telling them they need to solve their own problem is enough. "You can come to group time, when you have resolved your argument." But don't ignore atrocious behav-ior either, because the child looks to us for guidance.

CHAPTER 8
Proper and Improper Adult Reactions to Misbehavior

A child's upbringing is enormously impactful, which is why adults need to do the best they can to help him learn right from wrong, but the child is ultimately responsible for the decisions he makes and the type of person he becomes. The adult's responsibility lies in helping the child learn how to make good choices. Parents and teachers who accept the premise of the determinists, that the child does not have a free will, do not hold the child responsible for his own behavior. Instead, they think the responsibility for the child's behavior rests with other people. Therefore, when the child misbehaves, or even has a negative response to discipline, they may react with guilt, denial, anger, and/or fear. These responses can result in the adult implementing improper discipline or avoiding discipline altogether.

Guilt. There are two types of guilt: earned and unearned. Earned guilt is felt by people who know they committed a wrongdoing, but the guilt can be an impetus to learn how to improve one's behavior. Unearned guilt is felt by people who think they have done something wrong, but haven't. Unearned guilt can be crippling emotionally. It isn't possible to make amends for a wrong that wasn't committed, so the feeling of guilt remains unresolved. Unearned guilt affects discipline negatively.

Parents who think they are responsible for their child's misbehavior usually have trouble disciplining their children due to unearned guilt. While this can happen to anyone who does not hold the child accountable for his behavior, it is common with parents of children who have serious behavior problems. Stanton Samenow is an American psychologist whose specialty is criminal behavior. In his book, *Before It's Too Late, Why Some Kids Get Into trouble—and What Parents Can Do About It*, he explains why parents feel guilty because of their child's behavior:

> Guilt can be the most devastating emotion, for it often paralyzes parents so that they are unable to take effective action. As they struggle to make sense of it all, the mothers and fathers of these youngsters are positive they must have done something horribly wrong that caused their children to become so irresponsible. But rarely is this the case.
>
> It is tragic that for decades, psychiatrists, psychologists, social workers, and educators have convinced parents that they are chiefly responsible for shaping their children's destiny. Erroneously, the experts have asserted that the child comes into this world much like a totally unformed lump of clay and then is haplessly molded by parents. Millions of mothers and fathers have internalized this message and, understandably, feel blameworthy for everything that goes wrong. [1]

Manipulative children who sense the vulnerability of their parents can then take advantage of the situation to justify their misconduct. They accuse the parents of being oppressive or of committing immoral acts. Or they blame them and the family for their misbehavior. [2] The parents, convinced that they are to blame, become more upset with themselves than with their child.

Divorced parents usually suffer from guilt due to the sadness the children feel about the separation. Then parents worry that if they discipline their children it will make things worse, and neither parent wants to be viewed as the "bad guy." But discipline will *not* make it worse; it will make it better, because children feel more safe

---

1 Stanton Samenow, *Before It's Too Late*, (New York: Three Rivers Press, 2001) p. 13.
2 Stanton Samenow, *Before It's Too Late*, (New York: Three Rivers Press, 2001) pp. 11–24.

and protected when given limits. The child's world may have been shattered, and he certainly needs lots of comfort during that time, but sheltering him from his mistakes will not help him to mature. Parents do their children no favors by giving them the unsaid message that they themselves brought so much misery into the child's life that he now needs coddling forever. That is not giving the child any credit for being able to learn how to handle hardships and grief; the implication is that the child is weak.

In order to eliminate unearned guilt, the adult must hold correct moral standards such as teaching the child to do the right thing even if it causes him some temporary distress. But when an adult thinks the standard is to never let a child be unhappy, the parent feels guilty if the child cries when disciplined. The parent then ends up catering to every whim of the child so that the child never gets upset. The result is that the child learns that there are no standards for morality except how he feels at any given moment. The child does not learn that there is a real world out there and that to thrive in life you have to learn to think, to learn from mistakes, and to act based on moral principles. The child learns to act on his emotions of the moment, rather than reason, and expects everyone to cater to his emotions. If you are a parent, don't let unearned guilt motivate you to do the wrong thing. If you are a teacher, handle families suffering from guilt with sensitivity, but, at the same time, be honest with them about the child's need to be disciplined. [3]

Denial. Denial is an attempt to avoid pain by evading the reality of the child's behavior. When parents are told about their child's egregious behavior at school, those in denial typically have these reactions: "My child never lies." (In other words, he never does anything wrong.) Or, "Well, he doesn't act like this at home." (So it must be the school's fault.) And, "But he is so smart." (Therefore, he couldn't possibly be having behavior problems.)

My child never lies. The parent is being unrealistic. As explained in Chapter 3, children will sometimes lie for cognitive reasons, but if a child lies on purpose in order to fake reality, he needs immediate correction. The parent who defends that child may be attempting to

---

3 Children of divorce may also need counseling because they often feel that they somehow caused the separation.

evade the seriousness of the misbehavior. Or she might be trying to project herself as the perfect parent.

He doesn't act like this at home. In some cases, parents claim that their child is well-behaved with them, but it is hard to believe that parents could be so unaware of a child with serious behavior issues. Then, in different conversations, it slips out that they are having difficulties with their child, and they don't even seem to be aware that they have contradicted their former claim. On the other hand, maybe the parents are telling the truth, maybe the parents have never told him "no," and the child gets his way all the time. If this is the case, the parents have done their child a huge disservice. The real world doesn't operate without restrictions and rules. A child cannot be allowed to destroy property and go after other people with a vengeance. At any rate, it doesn't matter if he doesn't act like that at home; he acts that way at school.

But he is so smart. This is an excuse. Everyone has seen smart children. That doesn't mean all smart children feel good about themselves, that they can all concentrate, or that they take the initiative to learn. Education is a lot more than just knowing how to read or memorizing the multiplication tables. It is about teaching a child how to use his mind.

Just because someone is smart does not mean that person is well-behaved, moral, or can think logically. A con-man may be a good liar; a politician may be great at pulling the wool over the eyes of his constituents. Manipulators can be really smart and good at what they do, but they are reliant on controlling other people with deceit. This dependency will not lead to the development of self-respect and the resulting feeling of happiness.

A child may, indeed, be very smart and may have figured out that he has developed an ability to do and get what he wants without obeying the rules that have been set up to respect the rights of his classmates. All he has to do is manipulate others by lying and pressuring them into submission. If he comes to this conclusion, and continues interacting with people in this manner, it will become habitual and ingrained in his character. This will affect his entire life and the result won't be good. Intelligence is no excuse for poor behavior. Edwin A. Locke, Professor Emeritus, RH Smith School of Business, University of Maryland, states this concisely: "IQ does not give a child the right to be unethical. Moral principles apply to everyone, which the child needs to learn."

Some children as young as age three are headed for serious trouble,[4] and the resistance of some parents to face the fact that something is wrong with their child is understandable. It is upsetting. If you are a teacher and encounter parents who react with denial about their unruly child, try to communicate as effectively as possible the likely, ultimate results if the signs are ignored when reality inevitably rears its head down the line. Manipulative and insolent behavior must be stopped, and the sooner the better.

Anger. There is the misconception that showing anger to a child when he misbehaves is wrong because it would supposedly affect him negatively. People seem to think that in order to be a good parent or a good teacher, one must be forever patient, as if it is a sin to get angry.

When adults think anger is wrong, they suppress their true emotions and do not react genuinely, thereby not giving the child honest feedback for what he did. Some treat children with nothing but sugary sweetness and then suddenly explode when the child misbehaves. The adults think that if they just talk to the child, reason with him, the child will understand and cooperate. But the child does not understand, continues doing what he has been told not to do, and frustration keeps building up in the adult until it finally comes out in a burst of intense rage. Next comes the feeling of guilt, and the resolution to try harder to be patient with the child, and the process begins again. The child, on the other hand, is confused. No matter what he did, the adult accepted it, didn't do anything about it, then suddenly came down on him like an avalanche.

There are times when it is acceptable for the adult to express anger to a child because of misbehavior. The adult who understands the nature of the child feels patience in the majority of discipline situations. However, when a child does something destructive or harmful on purpose, thinks it is funny, or doesn't take it seriously and has a grin on his face, not only is it okay for the adult to get angry, it is appropriate to get angry. Haim Ginott, author of *Between*

---

4 At our school we saw children who needed psychological help prior to three years of age.

Parent and Child, explains, "In fact, failure to get angry at certain moments would convey to the child indifference, not goodness." [5] Contradictions such as this sabotage the child's ability to predict the future and to think long-range.

The child needs to know he did something egregious, and he judges by the adult's reaction how serious it was. (Just like I learned how serious it was to yank the steering wheel when my father was driving the car.) Not only does the child need to know the reasons why it is wrong, he needs to see how people react to what he did. Children need to learn that their behavior can affect other people and that one of the results might be anger.

Dealing with anger can be difficult. Ginott provides an answer as to why:

> In our own childhood, we were not taught how to deal with anger as a fact of life. We were made to feel guilty for experiencing anger and sinful for expressing it. We were led to believe that to be angry is to be bad. Anger was not merely a misdemeanor; it was a felony. [6]

Expressing anger doesn't mean flying into a rage, going into a rant, or threatening the child. Montessori was worried that there would be no defense for the child if the adult came down on the child in an angry, tyrannical way. Instead, you show on your face and in your tone of voice that you are upset. You state, "I am angry about this." Or, "I am very upset that that material was broken because of carelessness." Or, "I am feeling very frustrated that no one was listening to me." Children are honest, blunt creatures. If you want children to feel comfortable with you, you need to be honest with them. If a child does not take your anger seriously, point it out. "I'm not smiling. Look at my face. I'm angry."

If anger is expressed appropriately, the child sees that anger isn't anything to fear. He learns someone he trusts can be angry and he

---

5 Haim Ginott, *Between Parent and Child*, (New York: MacMillan Company, 1965), p. 50.
6 Haim Ginott, *Between Parent and Child*, (New York: MacMillan Company, 1965), pp. 48–49.

will still be safe, no one will get hurt, and the world does not come crashing down. In addition, the child learns from you that he can also be angry, and what better way for him to learn how to handle it than to observe how the adult handles it. "The child," wrote Ginott, "may learn that his own anger is not catastrophic, that it can be discharged without destroying anyone."[7]

Montessori recognized the importance of anger in the child's development:

> It often happens that children do not react violently. It might be better if they did, because the child who gets angry has discovered how to defend himself, and may then develop normally. But when he replies by a change of character, or by taking refuge in abnormality, his whole life has been damaged. Adults are unaware of this, and think there is nothing to worry about unless the child gets angry.[8]

There are many children who are afraid to admit they are angry because they think that anger is wrong. During hitting incidents, these children usually do not open up and explain what happened until they are told that it is okay to be angry. Anger is a healthy emotion in the face of injustice. Children should not be given the message that they shouldn't be angry. Anger isn't wrong; it just needs to be handled correctly.

Fear. Adults can be afraid to say "no" to a child for fear the child will have a tantrum or do something perverse, which may then require discipline. So in order to avoid discipline altogether, the parent lies to the child. I observed this at my school, Independence Montessori. The school was located in the basement of a church. When the parents came to pick up their children, they had to come down half a flight of stairs to the classroom. On their way out of the building, they passed a soda machine. Often children would ask their parents if they

---

7 Haim Ginott, *Between Parent and Child*, (New York: MacMillan Company, 1965), p. 52.
8 Maria Montessori, *The Absorbent Mind*, (New York: Dell Publishing Co., 1967), p. 132.

could have some soda, and many parents would tell their child that they didn't have any money. When the child is very little, he accepts the answer, but as he gets older he wonders about it. He is pretty sure his parent has money. He may have observed his dad buying gas that morning or saw money in Mom's purse. So he now begins to doubt himself. Since a child's relation to reality is unstable, he may conclude that something is wrong with him. He feels insecure. Therefore, lying keeps the child's mind in chaos and undercuts his development of self-confidence. In fact, lying to a child in order to avoid battles only postpones them. Eventually the child catches on that the adult is lying and can feel hurt, betrayed, and unloved. He comes to doubt the parent, which results in arguments and fights later on.

In addition, parents who lie to their children are teaching them that it is okay to lie. Parents are powerful role models, and children pay attention. When it comes to moral behavior, what parents do is more influential than what they say should be done. Children often lie if their parents lie. Instead of lying, parents need to tell their children "no" with the real reason why they can't have what they want to have. Telling a child "no" with a lie is detrimental to his development, and it is also detrimental to the child's relationship with the parent. It doesn't work in the long run.

Another tactic adults resort to, when they are afraid of the reaction of their children to discipline, is bailouts. Bailouts are done when the child makes a poor decision and the adult, rather than letting the child learn from his mistake, resolves it for him. The problem is that it teaches children that they don't have to be responsible for what they do. In one of the classrooms at our school, the children were required to bring in their snack before class time started. Inevitably, some children would forget and then complain later that they were hungry. In the beginning of the school year, they were reminded of the rule, but later on they were told that they were responsible for remembering, and, if they didn't bring their snack in, they would have to go without it. Some teachers had a hard time when a child was hungry and would go get it for him. A child isn't going be harmed because he misses a snack, but when he is bailed out, he will become dependent on the adult to do his thinking for him, not to mention that it does nothing to improve his memory skills.

Parents who are afraid that discipline will mar and upset their child do not want their child to be disciplined, but proper discipline does not cause harm to the child. Sarah was four years old, bright, happy, and inquisitive. She was a good child, enjoyable and fun, but she also had a mischievous streak. While sitting at group time in class, she would giggle and tickle the child sitting next to her or laugh and chat. Naturally this was disruptive and distracted the rest of the children in class when the teacher was giving lessons. So eventually Sarah was moved about three feet outside the group. She could still hear and participate, but it solved the disruption problem. The teacher told the parents what she had done and not to worry, that their child was not a discipline problem, that moving her was meant to help her settle down and pay attention to the presentations at group time. Sometime later her mom came to observe, saw Sarah sitting outside the circle and immediately removed her from the class. "I just felt so bad seeing her sit there behind the others."

About a year later Sarah came with her family to the annual Christmas program. When they arrived, the father immediately went over to the teacher and said, "Sarah could hardly wait to get here to see you." When Sarah saw her former teacher, she ran right up and gave her a hug. Throughout the night Sarah stayed with her teacher, chatting and laughing with her. When Sarah's parents pleaded repeatedly that she return to them, Sarah refused, insisting that she wanted to stay with her teacher.

About three weeks later the teacher received a scathing letter from the mother stating that the teacher had scarred Sarah for life because she had separated Sarah at group time. Sarah obviously did not feel the same way as her mother; she had not been hurt by the discipline.

Most children, like Sarah, actually appreciate correction. Firmness makes them feel secure. It is interesting to see that children who have been corrected and disciplined surround their teachers with love and affection. Montessori reported the same phenomenon.[9] Countless times at school children expressed pride to their parents about the fact that they had rules that they had to follow at school. Cassandra, age eight, expressed respect and admiration for her favorite babysit-

9 Maria Montessori, *The Discovery of the Child*, (India: Kalakshetra Publications, 1966), p. 86.

ter: "When Amy baby-sat us we couldn't get away with a *thing*. She used to sit with her back to us doing her homework. We figured she wasn't paying any attention so we would jump on the bed. As soon as we started jumping, she'd turn around and tell us to stop. She was so stern, but she was only stern about the things we *couldn't* do. She was very stern. Mom, I *really* liked her!"

Adults do not need to be afraid of implementing honest, straightforward discipline. It does not damage children; it helps them make better choices. Children recognize that the adult is trying to help them, and they like it…and appreciate it.

CHAPTER 9
Summary and Conclusion

Montessori's method of discipline is revolutionary because the goal is independence, not obedience. Rather than the adult controlling the child, the child learns how to control himself. He doesn't need to be constantly bombarded with commands from the adult on how to behave because he develops the ability to behave on his own. He develops self-discipline.

Children in genuine Montessori schools acquire independence for two reasons. First, based on Montessori's view that the distinguishing characteristic of humans is reason, Montessori figured out a way to help children think more clearly and accurately. She developed hands-on, self-correcting materials for the children to work with that focus on different aspects of reality. Secondly, the teacher monitors the progress of the children by making presentations of the materials, providing freedom within limits for the children to work and correcting misbehavior. By working with the materials, along with guidance and discipline from the teacher, the children improve their ability to reason and develop good behavior. To the extent that current Montessori schools consistently follow Montessori's original principles, these are the results they get.

There are reasons why behavior is getting worse at school, at home, and in public. Children can't help but be influenced by the culture in which they live. Our culture has been deteriorating due to the wrong idea that there are no objective moral values, that there is no objective truth. So rather than appealing to the child's reasoning ability and teaching him that there are objective rationales for proper behavior, the child learns that morality is determined by group agreement. Individuals need rational principles to guide their lives, not the opinions of others whose opinions are based on the opinions of others. The result is that rational principles become replaced with emotion. And so it is with discipline.

There is another significant reason why the behavior of children is getting worse—the premise of determinism has been accepted and children are being treated as if they don't have free will. Children are not being held accountable for their behavior because "someone didn't treat him right." Or "he felt sad." Or "he has low self-esteem." Or "no one will play with him." And on and on. The assumption is that behavior is determined by social acceptance rather than the choices that the child makes. Therefore, the child must be kept happy all the time so that he feels accepted and will behave well. The result is that children are emotionally indulged instead of disciplined. In other words, they are spoiled.

In order to resolve the behavior problem, the differences in philosophic ideas need to be examined, because different views of human nature manifest in discipline. The view that humans do not have free will, and therefore behavior is determined by outside forces, leads to the type of discipline (or lack of it) advocated by Dewey, behaviorism, humanistic psychology and positive discipline. The view that humans have volition leads to the type of discipline advocated by Montessori. [1] When acts of misconduct are committed by children in schools and out in public, instead of examining these philosophical differences, people start pointing fingers. The parents blame the teachers and the teachers blame the parents. Who is to blame? The answer is both. To whatever extent educators and parents accept the wrong premises about human nature, they are to blame. The solution is to check and re-think those premises and treat children according to their true nature—which means to hold them accountable for the choices they make.

In closing, I want to share a true story that illustrates how impactful proper discipline can be on a child's life. Elizabeth was a bright, energetic child. From a young age she was very headstrong and

---

1 Since this book is about Montessori's method of discipline, I am only mentioning her method here.

determined, and also very emotional. She went to Montessori school, was an excellent student, and loved school. Her parents had always used the discipline techniques advocated in this book: consequences, time-outs, encouraging and allowing acceptable choices, etc., and they were always consistent in their follow-through. In ninth grade she left Montessori, went to a public school and began to go down the wrong path. She started to reject her parents and all the values they had tried to instill in her growing up. Trying to reason with her only ended in heartbreak and explosions. Nothing was working... so...they ramped up the discipline. They completely cut her off from her friends. Her father called the cell phone company and set it up so that the only people she could communicate with were family or 911. Then they took all their land line phones and locked them in their bedroom. A few months later Elizabeth and her mother went to their cabin for three weeks. They were there alone, just the two of them. One night, as her mother was reading in bed, Elizabeth knocked on her door.

"Mom, can I talk to you for a minute?"

"Sure."

"You know," she began, "when you and Dad cut me off from my friends, that was the *best* thing you ever did. Because then I no longer had to worry about what my friends thought about me. It took all the pressure off so I could just concentrate on myself and what *I* thought about me."

Her mother was stunned. Just a few months prior Elizabeth had screamed at the top of her lungs that they were the worst parents in the world, and she had fretted that Elizabeth was a lost cause. Now today, as an adult, Elizabeth tells her parents that they are her heroes because they didn't let her get away with her immoral behavior.

The reason children love it when adults set limits is because they feel cared about. "The adult cared enough about me to keep me safe and help me behave." But if the child is always presented with a positive view of himself, even when he is doing negative things, he isn't helped; he is actually hindered. How can we expect him to make a correction when he doesn't know he has done anything wrong? He has no way of distinguishing right from wrong and has no guidelines for changing.

Adults shouldn't give him the view that everything he does is wonderful, and they are lying to him if they do. It is not wonderful when he misbehaves. Part of growing up is learning how to deal with the fact that just because you feel like doing something doesn't mean it is okay to do it. By not saying "no," adults send a child the message that everything in life will go as he wants no matter what he does. That isn't reality.

When a child doesn't listen and continues to misbehave, the adult has to take action. Then the child learns consequences: if I do "a," then "b" will happen. Consistency and follow-through teaches the child logic. When misbehavior is ignored, children learn to evade the obvious facts of reality, to pretend they don't exist rather than dealing with them forthrightly. When a child does not focus on learning the facts of reality, he doesn't learn how to think. Instead, he learns to operate on his emotions rather than rational thought. When the nature of the child is ignored, his growth is stunted. The risk is insecure, out of control, disrespectful children.

Montessori had the right view of both the child's nature and the role of the adult in guiding him towards independence. Therefore, her view of discipline was correct and is still correct today. The proper approach to discipline is not to make a child feel that you don't love him, but that you love him enough to take the actions required for him to learn the difference between right and wrong. Saying "no" to a child is not wrong, it is right, because discipline is not a bad word. Discipline is effective when done the Montessori way.

How to Communicate Effectively When Disciplining

- **Be direct.** Look directly into the child's eyes. With children you have to be as clear and direct as possible.
- **State the facts.** Name it outright. Children like directness and honesty; they don't understand subtleties. This doesn't mean that an adult should be harsh or unkind. Honesty and kindness are not mutually exclusive. The adult should just state the facts as a way of correction. "You hurt him when you pushed him down. See? He's crying." "Pushing other children is not allowed." "It is taking way too long to put your work away." "You are fooling around." "You are still running after I told you to stop." "Feet do not belong on the table." "No, you may not do that." "Yes, you did hit him. I saw you."
- **Give the child the word for the misbehavior.** "That was disrespectful when you stuck your tongue out at me." "That was rude when you put your hands over your ears when I was trying to talk to you." But don't tell him *he* is rude. There is a difference. Children are in the process of learning right and wrong. Just because he does something wrong now doesn't mean he will do it forever. You don't want him to think he has no control over what he does by stating a conclusion about his nature.
- **Be authentic.** Don't try to fake your displeasure with an insolent child. Some parents use an approach where the adult says in a sweet, gentle tone, oozing with goo: "Now Johnny. You know we don't do that." The adult was really angry, but covered it up by

trying to communicate love. Communicating love doesn't tell the child anything about his behavior. This approach teaches the child how to be a phony, and the child is confused. The tone of voice says "I love you," but the words are saying something else. Perhaps he should misbehave and the adult will love him? The adult should refrain from giving a child mixed messages and be honest when talking to him. If she isn't, he will know it and learn to ignore her.

- **Use a firm tone of voice**. A firm tone is different than an angry or a mean one. A firm tone means you are serious, that you mean it. It means that if they don't listen to you, consequences will be forthcoming.
- **Use "I-messages" whenever possible.** "I like the way..." "I want..." "I'm looking for..." "I'm waiting..." "It's my turn to talk." Using "I-messages" correct or direct children in a positive manner. "I like the way Miranda is sitting quietly during story time," often encourages the rest of the children to observe Miranda and then apply the information: "Am I sitting quietly?"
- **Speak in a way that encourages the child to think:** "What did I say? Try to remember." "And now what are you supposed to do?" "Show me that you are ready to go." "Show me how to sit properly." "What should you be doing now?" "You don't need to tell me. Show me." "Where do you belong?"
- **Point out the positive.** "You've done a lot of work today. I bet that feels good." "I like the way Jenna is sitting with her legs crossed and her hands in her lap. She is ready to go outside." "I see a sparkling clean table."
- **Raise your voice, if needed**. Many people think that adults should never raise their voices when speaking to children. It depends. It can be done to get their attention or so they can hear you in certain circumstances such as potentially dangerous situations. Raising your voice is different from yelling. (Yelling is usually used in anger, although there are some circumstances where it is used for the same reasons.) You don't want to fill a child with anxiety, giving him the notion that he can't do anything right, so only raise your voice when circumstances call for

it. (Montessori noted that there are times when it is appropriate for the teacher to raise her voice.[1])

- **Listen to the child.** Avoid comments like, "Is that anything to cry about?" "We don't say hate." "That's nothing to be afraid of." Statements such as this only serve to get the child out of touch with his thoughts and feelings and make problems harder, if not impossible, to solve. Try to understand what he is actually saying or asking. When a child says, "I hate Audrey," he is really saying that he is angry. If adults come down on him because he used the word "hate," he will think the emotion of anger is not permissible. Say, "You sound really angry with her right now. What happened? Want to talk about it?"

- **Reflect the child's feelings.**[2] Acknowledge and respect his feelings when he comes to you upset. "When I was a child that bothered me too." "I can see why that bothers you. I'd be upset too." "You are angry that he took the ball away from you." "You want Julia to play with you and you are upset because she wants to work with someone else."

- **Help him understand and deal with his feelings.** Emotions are automatic reactions that come from cognitive appraisals. For example, anger is due to an appraisal of injustice. Teach the child that just because he feels an emotion doesn't mean he has to act on it. "I see how upset you are, and I don't blame you, but it was wrong to hit him." If the child contributed to the problem because of inappropriate actions when he was feeling angry, talk with him about a better way to handle the situation. Also, help him to understand that feelings are not the same thing as facts. "I understand why you are scared and don't want to go to bed, but look, see? There is nothing under your bed."

---

1 Maria Montessori, *The Absorbent Mind*, (New York: Dell Publishing, 1967), pp. 268–269. "It is for her to judge whether it is better for her to raise her voice amid the general hubbub, or to whisper to a few children, so that the others become curious to hear, and peace is restored again."
2 Haim Ginott, *Between Parent and Child*, (New York, Macmillan Company: 1965), pp. 17–36.

APPENDIX 2—for Parents
Suggestions for Establishing Consequences

Some parents told me they had trouble thinking of consequences for their children's misbehavior and asked if I would make a list of suggestions. Bear in mind that these are merely suggestions and will not necessarily work for every child. You have to find what works for *your* child. Successful discipline and thinking of effective consequences is something you can learn, and it gets easier with practice. Note: Some of these ideas are not actually consequences, but rather techniques to help the child focus better (such as re-presenting a lesson or comforting the child).

Listed are various suggestions that have been successful for some families. They are organized by category. The main discipline issue involved is listed, even though other issues may also be present. Hopefully, this will help you to think of principles when disciplining your child (e.g., serious safety issues need to be dealt with quicker than social issues), and therefore will make it easier for you to think of an appropriate consequence.

RUDENESS

Not being quiet or settling down when asked: TESTING ISSUE
- Time-out. (I recommend this a lot, but sometimes taking away a privilege is just as good.)
- Send to his room.
- Put the child on "silence."

"Bugging"—purposely irritating another person by mimicking, staring, shadowing, touching, etc.: SOCIAL ISSUE
- Time-out.
- Isolation.

Name Calling: SOCIAL ISSUE
- Time-out.
- Put child on "silence."
- Isolation.

Offensive words or inappropriate words: TESTING ISSUE
- Time-out.
- Isolate from others.
- Put on "silence."
- Remove a privilege (i.e., no television, no treat, or no bike riding).

Interrupting: SOCIAL ISSUE
- Give the child a demonstration on how to get someone's attention, then invite the child to practice.
- Tell the child you are going to ignore him until he tries to get your attention politely.

STEALING OR TAKING A PROHIBITED ITEM

Child takes something that he knows doesn't belong to him: MORALITY ISSUE
- Explain to the child what stealing is and why it is wrong. Have child return the item to its owner.
- Child works to earn money to replace item.
- For repeated offenses you might want to consider taking the child to the police station and request their help.
- The child writes (or dictates to the parent) why stealing is wrong. He could give three reasons why he wouldn't want someone to steal from him.

Sneaking candy and/or snacks or activities like video games, etc.: MO-RALITY ISSUE

- Remove whatever was taken and ban the child from it for a period of time.
- Increase time if it happens again. You could also take away television privileges or the video games.

Using another person's belongings without asking: MORALITY ISSUE
- Teach the child how to ask for permission.
- Time-out.
- Items are taken away from that child and returned to the rightful owner, or make the child return them.

Knowingly drinking someone else's juice or eating someone else's snack: MORALITY ISSUE
- Ban the child from snack for the rest of the day. Next offense, one week.
- Take away his snack.

DEFIANCE

Child hits parent: MORALITY ISSUE
Do not allow this! It is psychologically damaging for a child to hit his parent whom he loves.
- Grab and hold the child so he can't hit you.
- Firmly move the child to an isolated place and emotionally show your anger. Say, "I am very angry with you!" and look at him sternly. Leave him to sit there alone for a while. Later explain to him what happens in the outside world when people do that.

Refusal to accept responsibility for his actions i.e. clean messy room: TESTING ISSUE
- Is the child feeling overwhelmed by the mess? Children age five and younger may need some help. Sort items into piles so that the child can put things away more easily. Also, provide room with shelves (instead of toy boxes) and containers to put possessions in. Be prepared to go in with a shovel once in a while.

- "We can't go to the park until your room is clean."
- "If it's not done by dinnertime, you'll eat alone." (State when dinnertime is and give some frame of reference.)
- Set a timer. Tell him if his room is picked up by the time the timer goes off, he can play a game with you.
- Try some humor. One father told me that when his daughters didn't want to clean their rooms he would say in a silly tone, "Vat doesn't keel you will make you strooong."

Flat out refusal to put on shoes, coat, etc.: TESTING ISSUE
- Tell him you're going to count to ten and if his shoes and coat are not on by then, he will sit in time-out.
- Count to ten and if it isn't done, put him in the car without his shoes and coat. Then don't turn the heat on and let him see what it feels like to be cold (not too cold, just so he is uncomfortable).
- Let him walk on the cold pavement (providing it won't be harmful).
- Walk out to the car without the child. Have another adult escort the child to the car.
- Put your hands on the child's hands, put the child's hands on the coat or shoes and move him through the motion of putting the item on.

Talking back, speaking disrespectfully, or even laughing in defiance: TESTING ISSUE
- Be very firm, send to time-out with a firm voice. Tell him it isn't funny.
- Take child by the hand to time-out without a word, then ignore.
- When he comes to ask you for a favor later ("Can you take me to the park?"), refuse and remind him that he didn't treat you with respect and you don't do things for people who aren't nice to you.
- Send him to his room.
- Remove privileges.
- Have the child write (or dictate to a parent) about the meaning of respect.

Screaming and refuses to stop: TESTING ISSUE
- "You have two choices. You can either stop screaming or go to your room."

Child keeps screaming and refuses to go to his room: TESTING ISSUE
- Carry or escort the child to his room.

Child refuses to stay in room: TESTING ISSUE
- Hold the door closed. Tell the child in a calm voice that you will let go when he stops screaming and stays in his room.

DANGER

Standing or jumping on furniture: SAFETY ISSUE
- Time-out.
- Ban the child from sitting on furniture and at mealtime the child has to stand while eating. (Most effective.)

Crossing the street without looking: SAFETY ISSUE
- Ban the child from crossing the street for a period of time.
- Ban the child from crossing the street without an adult escort.
- Ban the child from going outside.
- Have the child write (or dictate to a parent) about danger.

Hitting, pushing, shoving, biting: SAFETY ISSUE
- Time-out.
- Remove him from whomever he is hurting and isolate.

Playing with matches or other fire related behaviors: SAFETY ISSUE
- Take away the matches and put the child in time-out.
- Take away privileges.
- Practice fire drills. Ask him how he would feel to lose all his favorite stuffed animals, toys, etc.
- Show him a picture of a burn victim.
- Take the child to a fire station and ask the professionals to help you.

PROCRASTINATION

Avoiding completing a task or project: TESTING ISSUE (unless he needs help)
- Is the child watching television or doing something else instead? Tell him he can't watch television until the task is completed.
- Maybe he feels overwhelmed. Teach him to take it a step at a time. Perhaps he could take a small break in between steps.
- Give the child a certain amount of work that has to be finished by a certain time.

Dawdling in the morning and not getting dressed for school: TESTING ISSUE (unless he is ill, upset about something, etc.)
- Establish a routine of getting dressed, eating breakfast, and then brushing teeth. Consistent routines can help the child to stay on track.
- Count to ten. If his clothes aren't on, put him in time-out.
- Tell the child you will take him to school in his pajamas if he is not ready by the time you are ready to leave. Then do it.

LYING

Five-year-old tells huge story that his parents are adopting a baby boy: SOCIAL ISSUE
- Children this age are unclear about the difference between reality and fantasy. Respond, "You would really like to have a brother, wouldn't you?"

Child claims he didn't break a rule and you know he did: TESTING ISSUE
- Time-out.
- Remove privileges.
- If the child is hoping to change reality with this lie, don't let him get away with it. Remind him that what he is saying is not the truth and telling you something else will not change that.
- The child writes (or dictates to the parent) about lying and gives three reasons why it is wrong.

- Try to think of a consequence related to his lie. For instance, the child lies and says he cleaned up his mess so he can go outside and play. As soon as you discover his lie, make him come inside, finish cleaning the mess and sit in time-out. Then he may not go outside for the rest of the day.

The child claims he is ill so he won't have to go to school: MORALITY ISSUE
- If you are unsure if he is really sick, take him home, but he has to stay in bed all day.
- If you are sure he is trying to avoid school, try to determine why and get the problem resolved. If he is avoiding school because he wants to be home with you, take him to school without any hesitation.

PROPERTY

Children fighting over possessions: MORALITY ISSUE
- Don't force them to share.
- Label possessions.
- Don't have community toys (toys they all own together). If there is something you intend for all of them to use, such as a swing set or a board game, let them know it belongs to you and that you get to decide the rules regarding it. If they fight over it, you can tell them to resolve it or no one gets to use it.
- Have mats or rugs that children use to put their toys on like they do in Montessori school. Mats or rugs designate their individual work or play areas, and may alleviate some or all of the fighting.
- Before other children come over to play, ask your children to put away any items that they don't wish to share.
- Have a cupboard, shelf, or box that contains items that *you* share with visiting children.

The house is a mess and the children have a hard time picking up: MORALITY ISSUE (property respect)
- Have realistic expectations. Children and an immaculate household do not go hand in hand.

- Try to have a routine so they know when it is time to clean up. On Sunday nights, for example, they can watch a movie or play a board game once their jobs are done, baths taken, teeth brushed, and belongings picked up and put away.
- Give a list of what needs to be done by each child. Give the same number of jobs to each child, but you can give some of the harder jobs to the older children.
- Try to get in the habit of responding to requests ("Will you take us to the library?") with, "I'll consider it when the house is picked up."
- Put toys left out in a basket. The child has to earn them back before playing with them again.
- Some parents even throw away toys that aren't put away. I have never done this, but I heard it works great. Tell them if you end up cleaning the mess, you get to throw away whatever you want.
- Hands-on-hands approach. (Put your hands on the child's hands and walk him through the activity.)
- Verbally categorize directions for the children. "Pick up all your books." "Pick up all your stuffed animals." "Now pick up all your dolls." "Pick up all the doll clothes." "Pick up the tinker toys." (Go from large items to small items.)
- Have a family meeting to discuss this problem.

Slamming door: MORALITY ISSUE (property respect)
- Slowly show the child how to open and close the door quietly. Then invite him to try.
- Have the child come back and do it again the right way.
- If he already knows better, put him in time-out.
- Forbid the child to use the door, in which case he can't go outside to play.

MEALTIME PROBLEMS

The child refuses to eat: SOCIAL ISSUE
- Tell him he has to sit with the family, but doesn't have to eat if he doesn't want to. When the family is done eating, put his dinner

in a Tupperware container and put it in the refrigerator. He can eat it later, but no snacks or dessert until it is gone.

The child refuses to eat needed nutritional food: HEALTH/SAFETY ISSUE
- Tell the child no dessert until he eats a good meal. Give him guidelines (e.g., a protein and a fruit or vegetable).
- Explain to the child that as he grows up, his taste buds will change so he needs to at least taste everything or no dessert.
- Don't serve the child any of that food, but you serve everybody else that food. You continue to do that until the child asks for that specific food or, "How come I didn't get any?" Then just give him a dab of it until he asks for more.

Fighting at the dinner table: SOCIAL ISSUE
- "You have two choices. You can resolve your differences now or go to your room while we finish eating."
- Put children on "silence."
- "You must stop eating until the fighting is over."
- Turn their chairs so they face away from the table.

Running around at dinnertime: SAFETY ISSUE
- "Next time you get out of your chair, you're done." If the child gets out, the adult removes his food without a word. He will have to wait to eat sometime later.

Rudeness such as saying "yuck" to a meal: SOCIAL ISSUE (manners)
- Tell the child he can say once in a nice tone of voice, "I don't care for this." He may only say it one time. If he continues to say "yuck," remove his food and don't give him anything else to eat until sometime later. (Usually you have to do this only once.)

IN THE CAR

Bugging a sibling, yelling, kicking seats, etc. and not stopping when asked: SAFETY ISSUE
- Put on "silence."

- If possible, make the offender sit alone.
- Put the child in time-out when you get home.
- When you are one to two blocks away from home, have him/them get out and walk the rest of the way (provided it is in a safe area, and make sure you ride alongside in the car or can see him/them the entire time.)
- Pull the car over to the side of the road and don't say a word until the commotion stops. (Surprise Consequence.)
- If they like to listen to music in the car, turn it off. (Surprise Consequence.)
- Withdraw privilege such as riding a bike when you get home.
- Don't stop at the library, candy store, etc. if you had planned to do so. (Surprise Consequence.)

PROBLEMS IN PUBLIC

Misbehaves in restaurant: SOCIAL ISSUE
- Put on "silence."
- Get up and leave. (Have waiter box your food and pay for it as you leave.) When you get home do not serve it to the children. Send them to their rooms and let them eat something else later. You could also have them watch you eat first, if you are especially angry.
- Next time they ask to go out, refuse and ask them why you are saying no.
- Go out to eat at their favorite restaurant without them. Make sure they know it and briefly explain why they aren't being included.
- The child writes (or dictates to the parent) about proper behavior in restaurants.

Child breaks property: MORALITY ISSUE
- The child must admit what he did to the owner.
- The child must repair item.
- If the object must be replaced, the parents need to provide a way

for the child to earn money at home. The child must work and earn money for its replacement and take it to the owner.

Misbehavior or sassing back while shopping: TESTING ISSUE
- Time-out in the store or in the car.
- Leave the store and take the child home without a word (Surprise Consequence). No treats when you get home. (Most parents find this effective after just one trip home.)

The child loses his possession in store after you suggested he leave it in the car: TESTING OF REALITY ISSUE
- Accompany the child back to the store to look for toy.
- Explain why children should not take their things into the store, because sometimes they get lost.
- Do not buy a toy to replace the lost one; the child must earn his own money to replace it.

TEMPER TANTRUMS

The child is tired, hungry or sick: SOCIAL OR SAFETY ISSUE
- Hold, rock, or comfort

The child's sense of order is upset: SOCIAL OR REALITY ISSUE
- If possible, try to change environment so that things will be back to normal. If not, calmly reassure the child that things are okay.

Child wants to change reality or get his way: TESTING ISSUE
- Do not give in! If you do, he will learn that all he has to do is stomp his feet and he will get his way in the world. Send him to his room and tell him he can come out when he calms down. Then ignore him until the tantrum stops.

The adult is doing for the child what he can already do for himself. The child wants independence: (The adult is putting on the child's coat and the child has a tantrum): SOCIAL ISSUE
- Apologize and allow the child to do it himself.

BEDTIME DIFFICULTIES

The child won't get ready for bed: TESTING ISSUE
- Hands-on-hands approach. (The parent puts his hands on the child's hands and walks him through the activity.)
- Set a timer. No bedtime story if he is not ready when the timer goes off.
- Count to ten. Have a consequence ready if he isn't done by the time you get to ten.

The child won't stay in his room: TESTING ISSUE
- Tell him to get in bed and stay there or you will remove his music device or favorite stuffed animal.
- Keep returning him to his room. This may take several nights before he stays in his bed.
- Is he scared? Provide night lights, calm music, etc., or think of another solution to make him more comfortable.

The child won't go to sleep: SAFETY/HEALTH ISSUE
- Maybe he is not sleepy. Give him time to unwind with music or books. He should learn to do this on his own, however, and stay in his room or in bed.
- Eliminate afternoon nap.

MANIPULATION ATTEMPTS

Saying "I don't love you": TESTING ISSUE
(Note: The child is using this as a ploy to get you to give in so he will get his way. It is the same principle as the adopted child who said, "My mommy in Korea would let me do that." Or the child of divorced parents who claims the other parent would allow him to do what he wants to do. The child is trying out different methods, hoping he will hit upon the right one so he can do what he wants.)
- Do not let this bother you. If it does, don't show it! Respond with, "I'm sorry you feel that way because I love you. However, you still have to sit in the chair."

Pouting, baby talk, whining: SOCIAL ISSUE
- Refuse to respond to the child until he stops.
- Time-out.
- Mirror or imitate the child so he can see what he looks like. (Some children will think this is funny, some won't.)
- Have the child look in a mirror to see what he looks like when he pouts.
- "I don't listen or talk to whining or baby talk."

Excuse-making, such as "I didn't mean to." "I didn't know." "I was just kidding." "It just happened." "It is his fault." "He started it." "So and so told me to do it." "John did it so why can't I?": MORALITY ISSUE
- Confront the child with the truth. Don't let him get away with this. Follow through with a consequence anyway.

Shopping around for the answer he wants (Mom says no so the child asks Dad): MORALITY ISSUE
- Tell the child that the answer is an absolute "No," along with the loss of a related privilege.

APPENDIX 3—for Montessori Teachers
Discipline During Class Time

Here are some techniques for handling behavior issues during class time. All children are individuals and what works for one child may not work for another, but once you find out what works, be consistent and follow through. Keep in mind that when a disruption occurs, the children are watching you to see how it is handled and will make judgments about morality as a result.

TIME-OUTS

Sending a child to time-out. When a child misbehaves, do not give him too many chances before sending him to time-out. Continuous warnings are ignored by children. Do not give him more than three warnings and, depending on the child and the situation, only one warning may be sufficient. If the child already knows the rule and breaks it repeatedly, zero warnings are acceptable. Whether or not he sits next to you will depend on the circumstances and the type of child you are dealing with. Use your best judgement.

While in the break chair, the child should be left alone. His classmates should not talk to him, and the staff should focus their attention on the rest of the children who are working. If something special happens while a child is in time-out, such as another child serving an apple, he misses out.

Do not coddle a child when he is in time-out! The only exception to this is a child who is extremely sensitive, has never been in trouble before, and seems unusually distressed. For a child like that, it is permissible to reassure him that he is okay and, when he calms down, the two of you will talk about it. A brief comforting hug may be appropriate, but then leave.

GROUP OR CIRCLE TIME [1]

- All the children are required to attend. Everyone needs to learn how to sit quietly in a meeting and pay attention. In addition, children who do not come are a distraction. (There are some exceptions to this, of course. There are some group activities where children can be given a choice as to whether or not to attend. But exceptions should not be given for regular, routine group activities that involve the entire class.)
- If a new child is scared to come to group time, let him sit with you or an assistant. If he cries and the children start putting their hands over their ears, you might want to have the assistant take him out of the room and sit with him until he calms down. Sometimes reading him a book helps.
- The children need to sit on the line with their legs folded and their hands in their laps. (Or in any manner that helps with self-control, but I have found that this works best.) New children may not know how to fold their legs and may require help at first.
- Once the children sit down, they must stay in their spot and cannot get up without permission. Any drinks of water need to occur before they sit down.
- During circle time, the children need to be quiet. They may not interrupt the teacher.

Children are inattentive and noisy during circle time
- Give all the children assigned spots to sit on the line and separate the disruptive ones.
- For the child who is consistently disruptive, assign a spot outside the circle for him to sit.

---

1 Maria Montessori, *The Discovery of the Child,* (India: Kalakshetra Publications, 1966), pp. 79–80. Montessori talks about the value of arranging the children in order in their places for education or meetings involving the entire class.

- Make the disruptive child turn around so that his back is to the group.
- Count to 5, and whoever is talking by the time you get to 5 goes to a chair.
- "I like the way John has his hands in his lap and his legs folded."
- "Who knows how to sit the right way?" "I am looking for those children who know how to sit the right way. You don't need to tell me, just show me how nicely you can sit. John knows. Hazel is sitting properly. Look. She has her legs folded with her hands in her lap."

Children interrupt teacher
- Do not listen; tell the child to stop talking, but that he can talk to you during work time.
- If he doesn't stop, send him to a chair.

Noisy before music time
- Announce to the children that you are going to make a list of all the children who are sitting correctly. "I am going to read the names of the children who are on my list. When you hear your name you can stand up and you will be able to dance."
- Ring the bell.
- "I see (and then count) 1, 2, 3, 4, 5 children who are sitting the right way."
- "Show me that you are ready for music. If you're talking, you're not ready. Gabe, are you ready?" Or if they continue to talk, "Gabe isn't ready for music."
- Do not start the music until everyone is sitting quietly with legs folded and hands in their laps.
- "I can't start the music yet. It is way too noisy."

Children are not sitting properly and are waiting to be dismissed.
If your class ends with a group time, the children need to be still and quiet so that they can hear their names called when dismissed. If they have anything in their hands, such as a work paper, it needs to be placed on the floor. They must be silent, no clucking noises, no giggling, no noises with the lips, etc.

- Don't call on a child until he is sitting quietly and properly.
- Walk slowly around the circle and pause by each child who isn't sitting correctly. Adjust his legs if need be or send him to a chair.
- Name the specific children who are sitting properly. "John and Hazel are sitting correctly so they can get in line."
- "If you are talking, you're not ready." "If you are lying on the floor, you're not ready."
- "Where do your hands belong?" "What should you be doing?" When several children are being particularly noisy: "Bradley is not ready to go. Morgan is not ready. Bradley and Morgan, we are waiting for you." If they still ignore you, send them to a chair.

WORK TIME

Classroom is noisy
- Tell the entire class that they have to whisper. Anyone who talks goes to a chair or comes to sit next to you.
- Tell the children they are on "silence." When on "silence," they can't even whisper.
- Tell the specific children who are being loud that they have to whisper or are on "silence."
- Have noisy children come sit next to you.

Children wandering, not choosing work, or class is chaos
- "I'm looking for children who aren't working. Anyone who is wandering around the room will need to go to a chair."
- Use older or responsible children to help. "Can you help Johnny find something to do?"
- Use assistants to help. Show them how to present simple lessons like sandpaper letters or word analysis and then give them a list of children who need those presentations.
- "I'm going to count to 10 and I want to see everybody working. I will come around the room when I am done counting, and anyone who isn't working will go to a chair."
- Give a work list to the children who are wandering. When a child gets a list, he has to finish it. (Lists are only used temporarily until the child develops initiative. Some children like the idea

of lists and may ask for one, but if they are given a list, they need to complete it.)

- Assign individuals work. Tell them what work they need to take out and where you want them to do it.
- Tell the wandering children to take out a mat and they have to work there all day.
- Assign a disruptive child a designated work spot. Children may bring work to him at his assigned place. He may not leave that spot unless he has permission. If other children ask you about it, tell them we are helping him learn how to concentrate by giving him his own place to work.
- Ask a wandering child to help a friend.
- Time-out.
- Separate certain children.
- "Where do you belong?"
- "And now what are you supposed to do?"

Children don't stop when the bell rings
- Once you ring the bell during class time, don't do anything else until everyone in the room stops. If a child is moving, have an assistant walk over and stop the child. Call the child by name and tell him to stop, and don't continue until he does.
- If your class begins with group time, all the children must sit silently before going to work. No one can be dismissed until sitting properly. Learning this self-control prepares the child for stopping when the bell rings (and also the silence game).
- Practice at circle time. Demonstrate "stop" and have the children practice after you ring the bell.
- There is some great music that helps children learn how to stop, such as *The Freeze Dance* by Hap Palmer and *Stop and Go* by Ella Jenkins.

Abuse of material
- Re-demo.
- Make the child put it away.
- If it happens repeatedly, ban the child from using it until further notice.

Child refuses to finish work/stalls

- Try to determine why. Ask him if he needs help and help him if he needs it.
- If it is due to laziness, tell him he can't get up until the work is done (unless he has to go to the bathroom, get a drink, or eat lunch). If he doesn't finish by the end of the day, ask his parent at dismissal if she can wait. If not, make sure he gets it first thing the following day, and the same thing applies: he can't get up until it is done.
- Tell the child he is on a timer. (Or tell him he has until the clock says 2:00 to finish.) If it isn't done by the time the timer goes off, he will go to time-out.
- Don't let the child get away with making excuses. "I can't" and "I'm tired" often means, "I don't want to." Say, "You have to."

Child who is afraid to try

Gently encourage, but you may have to insist with hands-on-hands.

- Give him work that you *know* he can be successful with. When done, point out to him that he completed it by asking, "Who did that work?"

BIBLIOGRAPHY

Berliner, Michael, "Montessori and Social Development," *The Educational Forum*, March 1974.

Berliner, Michael, "Reason, Creativity and Freedom in Montessori," *The Educational Forum*, November 1975.

Berliner, Michael and Binswanger, Harry, "Answers to Common Questions about Montessori Education," *The Objectivist Forum*, vol. 5, June & August, 1984.

Bernstein, Andrew, "Why Students Can't Add or Subtract" https://www.capitalismmagazine.com/2002/01/the-new-math-why-students-cant-add-or-subtract/, *Miami Herald*, July 21, 2000; *Buffalo News*, August 13, 2000; *Charlotte Observer*, July 23, 2000; *San Jose Mercury News*; July 18, 2000; *Las Vegas Review-Journal*, July 24, 2000; *Spokesman-Review*, July 19, 2000.

Binswanger, Harry, "Logical Thinking," (paper presented at Objectivist conference, Williamsburg, Virginia), July 1–7, 1992.

Bradley, Michael, *Yes, Your Teen is Crazy*, Port Charlotte, Florida: Harbor Press, 2003.

Briggs, Dorothy, (paper on self-esteem presented at workshop, Tacoma, Washington), Spring 1982.

Bronson, Po, "How Not to Talk to Your Kids," http://nymag.com/news/features/27840/, New York News and Features, February 11, 2007.

Coe, Elizabeth Johnston, "Montessori and the Middle School Years," *Montessori and Contemporary Social Problems*, circa 1985.

Coloroso, Barbara, *Kids are Worth It: Giving Your Child the Gift of Inner Discipline*, New York: Harper Collins Publishers, 1994.

Cline, Foster and Fay, Jim, *Parenting with Love and Logic*, Colorado Springs, Colorado: Pinon Press, 1982.

Dewey, John, "Democracy and Education," https://archive.org/details/democracyandeduc00deweuoft/page/n159, p. 143.

Dewey, John, "Human Nature and Conduct," https://freeditorial.com/en/books/human-nature-and-conduct.

Dewey, John, "The School and Social Progress," *The School and Society*, Chicago: University of Chicago Press, 1907.

Dewey, John, "Reconstruction in Philosophy," https://freeditorial.com/en/books/reconstruction-in-philosophy.

Dobson, James, *Dare to Discipline*, Peabody, Massachusetts: Tyndale House Publishers, 1975.

Dreikurs, Rudolf, *Children: the Challenge*, New York: Plume, 1987; http://www.newworldencyclopedia.org/entry/Rudolf_Dreikurs.

Faber, Adele and Mazlish, Elaine, *How to Be the Parent You Always Wanted to Be* (audio cassette), New York: Simon & Schuster, 1999.

Faber, Adele and Mazlish, Elaine, *How to Talk so Kids Will Listen and Listen so Kids Will Talk*, New York: Avon Publishers, 1980.

Faber, Adele and Mazlish, Elaine, *Liberated Parents, Liberated Children*, New York: Avon Books, 1974.

Faber, Adele and Mazlish, Elaine, *Siblings without Rivalry*, New York: W. W. Norton and Company, 1987.

George, Marilyn, "Two- and Three-Year-Olds" and "Four-, Five-and Six-Year-Olds," Blue Gables Montessori School, Kirkland, Washington.

Ginott, Haim, *Between Parent and Child*, New York: MacMillan Company, 1965.

Glenn, Stephen and Nelson, Jane, *Raising Self-Reliant Children*, Rocklin, California: Prima Publishing, 1980.

Gordon, Thomas, *Parent Effectiveness Training*, New York: Peter H. Wyden Inc., 1970.

Healy, Jane, *Endangered Minds: Why Children Don't Think and What We Can Do About It*, New York: Simon and Schuster, 1990.

Healy, Jane, *Your Child's Growing Mind: A Guide to Learning and Brain Development from Birth to Adolescence*, New York: Broadway Books, 2004.

Hughes, Dr. Steve, "Good at Doing Things: Montessori Education and Higher Order Cognitive Functions," (paper presented at Bergamo Montessori School, Sacramento, California), http://www.goodatdoingthings.com/, September 1, 2012.

Kohn, Alphie, *Punished by Rewards*, New York: Houghton Mifflin Co., 1993.

Kramer, Rita, *Maria Montessori, A Biography*, New York: Capricorn Books, 1977.

Lillard, Paula Polk, *Montessori: A Modern Approach*, New York: Schocken Books, 1972.

LeShan, Eda J., *The Conspiracy Against Childhood*, New York: Atheneum, 1968.

Locke, Edwin A., *The Illusion of Determinism, Why Free Will is Real and Causal*, Maryland: Edwin A. Locke, 2017.

Maleskar, Kanchan, "Are You a 'Helicopter' Parent?" *Rediff News*, India, February 22, 2007, http://www.rediff.com/getahead/2007/feb/23parent.htm.

Montessori, Maria, *The Absorbent Mind*, New York: Dell Publishing, 1967.

Montessori, Maria, *The Advanced Montessori Method*, New York: Frederick A. Stokes Company, 1917.

Montessori, Maria, *The Discovery of the Child*, India: Kalakshetra Publications, 1966.

Montessori, Maria, *The Montessori Method*, Fresno, California: Schocken Books, Inc., 1964.

Montessori, Maria, *The Montessori Method*, New York: Frederick A. Stokes Company, 1912.

Montessori, Maria, *The Secret of Childhood*, New York: Fides Publishers, 1966.

Montessori, Maria, *The Secret of Childhood*, New York: Ballantine Books, 1966.

Montessori, Maria, *Spontaneous Activity in Education*, New York: Frederick A. Stokes Co., 1917.

Montessori, Maria, *Spontaneous Activity in Education*, New York: Schocken Books, 1965.

Montessori, Maria, *To Educate the Human Potential*, India: Kalakshetra Publications, 1948.

Neill, A. S., *Summerhill*, New York: Hart Publishing, 1960.

Nelsen, Jane, *Positive Discipline*, New York: Ballantine Books, 1987.

Nelsen, Jane, *Positive Discipline for Pre-Schoolers*, New York: Crown Publishing Group, 2007.

Neuman, Gary, *Helping Your Kids Cope with Divorce the Sandcastles Way*, New York: Random House, 1998.

Peikoff, Leonard, "Why Johnny Can't Think," *The Objectivist Forum*, Volume 5, Number 6, December 1984.

Rand, Ayn, "The Comprachicos," in *The New Left: The Anti-Industrial Revolution*, New York: New American Library, 1971.

Samenow, Stanton, *Before It's Too Late, Why Some Kids Get Into Trouble—and What Parents Can Do About It*, New York: Three Rivers Press, 2001.

Samenow, Stanton, *Inside the Criminal Mind*, New York: Crown Publishers, 1984.

Sears, William, "How to Say No," in *Ask Dr. Sears*, 2019, https://www.askdrsears.com/topics/parenting/discipline-behavior/how-to-say-no.

Standing, E. M., *Maria Montessori: Her Life and Work*, New York: New American Library, 1957.

Standing, E. M., *The Montessori Method, A Revolution in Education*, Fresno, California: Academy Library Guild, 1962.

Winn, Harbour, "A Child's Development of the Conceptualization of Time."

Walsh, David, *No: Why Kids—of All Ages—Need to Hear It and How Parents Can Say It*, New York: Simon and Schuster, 2007.

Walsh, David, *Why Do They Act That Way?: A Survival Guide to the Adolescent Brain for You and Your Teen*, New York: Free Press, 2005.

Wikramaratne, Lena, AMI Montessori Training Course, Palo Alto, California, 1972–1973.

Wolf, Anthony, *Get Out of My Life, But First Could You Drive Me & Cheryl to the Mall: A Parent's Guide to the New Teenager*, New York: Farrar, Straus and Giroux, 2002.

Wood, Paul, *How to Get Your Children to Do What You Want Them to Do*, (audio cassette) Pasadena, California: Cassette Works, 1977.

Zimmerman, Sarah Cole, (paper on self-esteem presented at workshop, Berkeley, California) Feb. 20, 1983.

About the Author

Charlotte Cushman is a Montessori educator with more than 40 years of teaching experience. She currently is a consultant for Montessori Renaissance Academy and speaks to parents, teachers, and the general public on Montessori and discipline.

She graduated from Lewis and Clark College, Portland, Oregon in 1972, with a B.S. Degree in Elementary Education. While attending college, she went on an overseas program to Japan where she did an independent study project, "Child Discipline in Japan." Immediately after graduation she took her AMI Montessori training at the Montessori Training Center, Palo Alto, California, from Lena Wikramaratne, a colleague and friend of Maria Montessori.

After that she worked as an assistant teacher at Golden Montessori, Portland, Oregon, moved back to the Midwest, and worked as the head teacher at Sunrise Montessori in Anoka, Minnesota. In 1985, she and her best friend, Carol Landkamer, started their own school, Independence Montessori. When Carol retired, Charlotte joined her husband's school, Minnesota Renaissance School, which he had started a few years prior.

She has authored two other books, *Montessori: Why It Matters for Your Child's Success and Happiness,* which explains the Montessori method; and a children's book, *Your Life Belongs to You,* a true story about the founding of the United States, which she taught to her students.

She has also authored numerous articles about child development and has been published in periodicals such as "Montessori Life," "The

Montessori Courier," "Public School Montessorian," "Minnesota Parent," "The American Thinker," and the newsletter, "Putting People First." She has delivered presentations to various community groups and numerous parent groups on child development, discipline, and the Montessori philosophy and method.

She is a parent and grandparent and enjoys spending time with her family at their cabin. She also enjoys sewing, quilting, reading, knitting, music, genealogy, traveling, talk radio, doll collecting, psychology, and discussing ideas.

9 780578 678542